Acting in Television Commercials

Acting in Television Commercials for Fun and Profit

Expanded and Updated

by SQUIRE FRIDELL

Illustrated by Barry Geller

HARMONY BOOKS / *New York*

For Suzy McDermaid. I love you.

Copyright © 1980, 1986 by Squire Fridell
Published by Harmony Books, a division of Crown
Publishers, Inc., 225 Park Avenue South, New
York, New York 10003 and represented in Canada
by the Canadian MANDA Group

HARMONY and colophon are trademarks of
Crown Publishers, Inc.
Manufactured in the United States of America

Library of Congress Cataloging-in-Publication
Data

Fridell, Squire.
   Acting in television commercials for fun
and profit.
      1. Acting for television—Vocational
guidance.   2. Television advertising—
Vocational guidance.
I. Title
PN1992.8.A3F7   1987   792′.028′023   86-19488

ISBN 0-517-56424-6
10 9 8 7 6 5 4 3 2 1

First Revised Edition

CONTENTS

ACKNOWLEDGMENTS

There are a lot of people to thank for helping me with this book. I hope these acknowledgments cover them all.

To my mom and dad, who somehow instilled a work ethic in me (without my knowledge).

To my wife, who never lets me settle for anything less than I should.

To my daughter, who makes me smile.

To my students over the years, who always ended up teaching me.

To Barry Geller, Harriet Bell, Melissa Schwarz, and Diane Cleaver for their hard work. To Pen Dennis, Dennis Gallegos, Jack Goldsmith, and the public-relations staffs at both SAG and AFTRA for helping me with information and the gathering of material.

To Maharishi.

Last, to everyone who hired me (and even to those who didn't, but thought about it . . .).

I can no other answer make but thanks, and thanks, and ever thanks.
William Shakespeare (and Squire Fridell)

AUTHOR'S NOTE

I began writing the first *Acting in Television Commercials* in 1977, thinking I had undertaken a three-month project. When the book was written, rewritten, re-rewritten, finally finished, and published three full years later in 1980, I vowed I would never, in this lifetime, put pencil—or eraser—to paper again.

Fortunately, or unfortunately, we human beings, unlike the more advanced animals, have a built-in ability to whitewash past unpleasantness and retain only a vague recollection of actual pain. It does appear that I have whitewashed any pain incurred during those difficult three years it took me to write my first book. I'm glad. This book needs to be written.

Those of you who are familiar with my first book will be pleased, I hope, with the new and updated information in this one. The Photograph, The Preparation and the Waiting, The Audition, and The Job have been greatly expanded. In the chapter on auditions, I've included dozens of suggestions for things you can do to ensure a call-back. All the other information in this book has been rewritten, updated, and revised, focusing on the actor who wants to work. As actors, that's the bottom line. We all want to work. Those of us who *do* work want to work more.

During the last six years since the first book came out, I've grown as an actor and as a teacher. I'm writing this updated edition to share what I've learned from acting in more than twelve hundred television commercials and teaching what seems like countless numbers of commercial acting classes. I hope you will profit by this new book.

My pencil is to paper. My eraser is at hand. Here goes again.

Squire Fridell

INTRODUCTION

Since 1941, when the first television commercial endorsing Bulova watches interrupted a baseball game (and probably annoyed the viewers), the television advertising industry has grown to a multibillion-dollar business. Strangely enough, in this day of consumer awareness and the shrinking dollar, the reason why most of us buy one product over another is because of the power of television and its ads.

For those few people who doubt the influence of the tube, the following statistics may change their mind:

• The average household in the United States has its TV set(s) turned on for six and a half hours a day. Up to seven minutes of every hour is devoted to selling something.

• More than three hundred dollars are spent each year on advertising for every man, woman, and child in the U.S. Most of that money goes to TV ads. This is an age when one million dollars are spent for 58½ seconds of advertising.

• From birth to age twenty-one, an average person in the U.S. sees at least a quarter of a million ads on television.

• By the age of three, a child in the U.S. will have seen more than twenty thousand television commercials.

• By the time a child enters kindergarten, he or she will have spent more time in front of the TV than will be spent in school for the next five years.

• By age eighteen, an average person in the U.S. will have spent a total of two years of his or her life in front of the television set.

• There are more TV sets in the U.S. than there are toilets.

Advertisers are well aware of the incredible power of television advertising. They are also aware that in order to advertise effectively, they need to use actors and actresses. The Screen Actors Guild has revealed a staggering fact: Commercials represent about half of the total income of all actors.

In simple terms:

Actors make as much money acting in television commercials as they make acting in movies and television combined!

However, a recent survey by the Screen Actors Guild revealed that while seventy-eight percent of the union listed their primary skill as "actor," only ten percent listed themselves primarily as "commercial actor."

In simple terms:

Only ten percent of the actors make fifty percent of the money!

FOUR REASONS WHY THESE STATISTICS ARE IMPORTANT AND WHY YOU NEED THIS BOOK

1. It will answer all the questions and clear up all the misconceptions almost everyone has about television commercials.

2. It will give the millions of viewers who have watched commercials and thought "Gee, I could do that," an honest look at their chances.

3. It is a step-by-step guide into the world of acting in television commercials for the beginning actor.

4. It is a comprehensive guide for the established actor who is working but wants to work more.

To find out if acting in television commercials might be the right choice for you, simply answer the questions in the following check test . . .

A TEN-POINT CHECK TEST FOR THE PROSPECTIVE COMMERCIAL ACTOR

	Yes	No
1. I would enjoy never knowing when I will work.	____	____
2. I would enjoy never knowing *if* I will work.	____	____
3. I would enjoy having difficulty establishing credit.	____	____
4. I would enjoy unemployment lines.	____	____
5. I would enjoy surly answering services.	____	____
6. I would enjoy not getting paid regularly.	____	____
7. I would enjoy having the grocery clerk ask his boss if it is okay to cash my personal check.	____	____
8. I would enjoy having my spouse (and my children) work to support me.	____	____
9. I would enjoy having a total stranger inform me that I look much heavier (and younger) on TV.	____	____
10. I would enjoy my mother's weekly telephone call to tell me I should have stayed in medical school.	____	____

If you answered yes to all the above, then you may proceed. Acting in commercials may be the right profession for you.

Admittedly, the preceding check test was written in fun, but the questions have some truth in them. Ask any actor.

There are facts that the prospective actor must be aware of before embarking on this *very* competitive career:

• There are a lot of people to compete with: SAG (Screen Actors Guild) membership is over fifty-eight thousand, and AFTRA (American Federation of Television and Radio Artists) members total sixty-five thousand (see The Unions).

• Seventy percent of the members of AFTRA and SAG have to hold down other jobs.

• Fifty-five percent of SAG members earn less than one thousand dollars per year.

• Seventy-five percent of SAG members earn less than thirty-five hundred dollars per year.

• Forty percent of all SAG earnings are made by one percent of the membership.

These facts point out rather dramatically that acting—whether it be in commercials, on TV, or in film—is a risky business for the wage earner. But, remember, no matter how discouraging the statistics revealed by the unions may be, success can be yours with the proper application of five major qualities:

1. Fairly acceptable, normal features (one nose, two eyes, etc.)

2. A degree of talent

3. An incredible amount of determination

4. Some training

5. Knowledge

The first two qualities are only slightly alterable; the second two are up to you. The careful application of this book is your key to the last.

Sounds good, but do I have to move to New York or Los Angeles to work?

That's a good question, and the answer is no. Certainly the majority of commercials (eighty-seven percent) are produced in New York and Los Angeles, but that also happens to be where most of the other actors (eighty-two percent) make their homes. There is a lot of advertising done in Chicago, San Francisco, Dallas, Phoenix, Seattle, Denver, Miami, Portland, Detroit, Atlanta, San Diego, Houston, Anchorage, Honolulu—almost every major city in the United States.

There are a lot of advantages to starting your career in acting in television commercials near your home town. You may be able to join the Screen Actors Guild easily, you won't have to pack up and move away from home, you will be able to keep your present job and dabble in commercials, and you may be able to supplement your income by thousands of dollars every year. (You also won't have to compete with eighty-two percent of the actors in the United States!)

What about making a living at other forms of acting in front of a camera?

Glad you asked. Here's the exact breakdown.

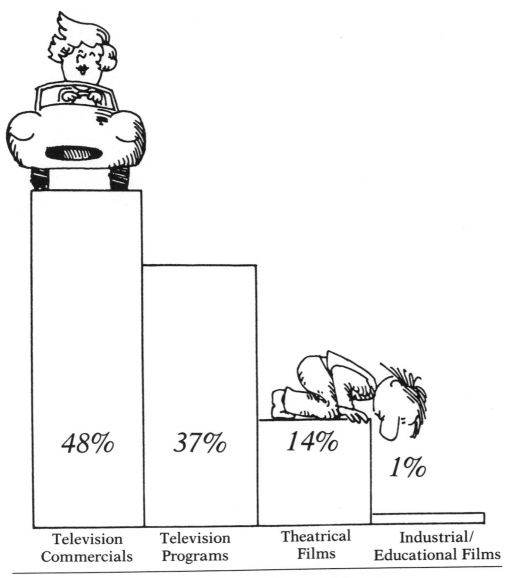

Television Commercials	Television Programs	Theatrical Films	Industrial/ Educational Films
48%	37%	14%	1%

Screen Actors Guild Distribution of Earnings

What about the breakdown by age, sex, and ethnicity?

Another good question!

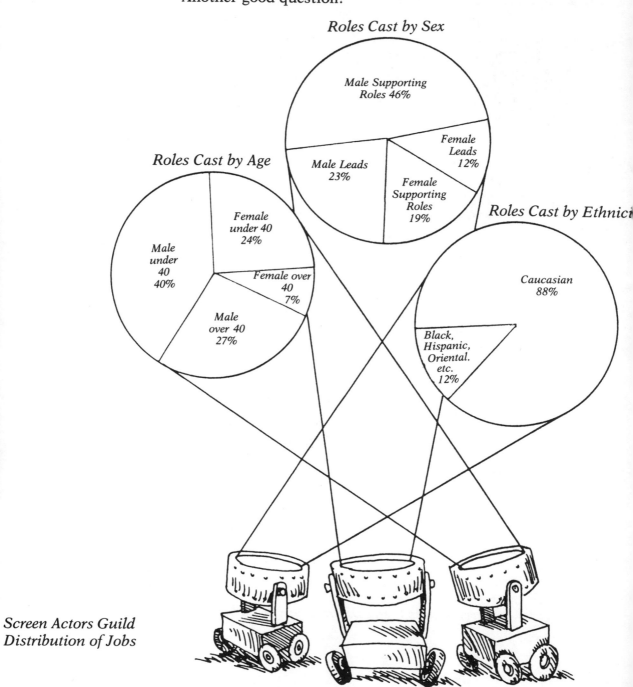

Roles Cast by Sex

Male Supporting Roles 46%

Female Leads 12%

Male Leads 23%

Female Supporting Roles 19%

Roles Cast by Age

Female under 40 24%

Male under 40 40%

Female over 40 7%

Male over 40 27%

Roles Cast by Ethnicity

Caucasian 88%

Black, Hispanic, Oriental. etc. 12%

Screen Actors Guild Distribution of Jobs

Now . . . with the proper application of this book, the road you travel in your pursuit of acting in television commercials will be directed toward the land of least mistakes.

The remainder of this book will be devoted to getting started. At this point we should introduce our two major characters, who could be you:

Arnold Anybody   Arlene Anybody

Follow them from this point on through the often confusing, usually perplexing, world of the commercial actor.

BEFORE THE AGENT

THE PHOTOGRAPH

Every actor in commercials, whether already established or just starting, needs photographs. Not only does he or she need photographs in the search for an agent, but to be successful, the actor needs *good* photographs.

The name of this game is *advertising*. You need to advertise yourself better than your competition. The average commercial agent is probably mailed or hand-delivered more than one hundred photographs, composites, snapshots, or slides each week, either from actors wishing to change agents or from aspiring actors hoping for a career in commercials. It takes that agent (or usually a secretary) about twenty seconds to sort through these pictures and select the four or five he or she feels might be worth taking a longer look at.

The purpose of this section of the book is to make sure your picture is one of the five chosen and not one of the ninety-five tossed in the garbage.

It should be mentioned here that your photograph should be an *exact* portrait of you and *how you look now*. Many people don't like having their picture taken or seeing themselves in a photo. This usually means they don't like what they see (or think they'll see). Before you have that first photo session, look in a full-length mirror and take a very critical, objective look at yourself.

• Look at your figure and any bulges that you don't like. Television adds a full ten pounds to everyone, so if you're just about right for your height, lose a little. You can never be too thin for television. Work out and tighten up.

• Take a look at your hair. Too long or too short is out. If you have bangs, it's important that your eyes can be seen. Long sideburns are out for men and so are toupees. It's better to be a little balding. If you are a graying twenty-five year old, dye your hair.

• Your hands must be presentable. If you bite your nails, stop. Your nails should be neatly trimmed and clean.

• Look at your teeth. Make sure they're straight and not discolored; if they're bad, have them fixed.

• If you wear glasses, think about getting contact lenses.

So, if you need to lose weight, have your hair done, have your nails repaired, get your teeth fixed, or get contact lenses, the time to do all those things is *now*—before that first photo session.

At this point in your search for an agent you need, what we call in the industry, a "head shot." Quite simply, it's an 8 × 10 photograph of your face. That sounds easy enough, except that very few people actually enjoy having their picture taken. It makes the best of us feel a little self-conscious, ill at ease, and tense. Photos don't lie. If we feel stress or tension, it stands out.

If you plan to have a professional photographer shoot your first pictures, be prepared. Actors seem to squander more hard-earned dollars on never-to-be-used pictures than on anything else. It's your money; spend it wisely.

Remember—you *are hiring* him *(not the other way around)!*

Make sure you meet the photographer before you pay for a shooting session. You should feel comfortable and relaxed with him. Look at his work and make triple sure you're satisfied. Shop around if you don't feel exactly right about him, or you'll be wasting your money.

Discuss beforehand exactly what you want him to do and what the pictures are for. Find out what his ideas are, where he plans to shoot, what clothes you should bring (colors, styles, number of changes), and what you should do about makeup and hair. The more you know *before* the shooting day, the more prepared and relaxed you'll be *on* the shooting day. Also remember that the night-before always shows up the day-after. Get a lot of sleep—and cancel the shooting if you've got a cold. (It will show.) Arrive early and don't schedule much else for the day. Leave yourself time.

I've found that it's a good idea to talk to the photographer during the session. Ask him about his career, his camera, whatever. You'll find that he'll take an interest in you, and he'll slow down a little. You'll get better pictures. Incidentally, I'd advise you to get a friend who has a 35mm. SLR camera to take some practice head shots before you pay a professional. Tell him what you want in a head shot, then go to a park and shoot a few rolls of black-and-white film. You'll gain experience and end up with a much better head shot later on.

How much money?

A good professional photographer should charge no more than $125 for shooting head shots. Included in that price are usually two rolls of black-and-white (don't use color) 35mm. film developed and printed

15

. . . by an animal

. . . or a group

. . . or another person

onto contact sheets. (Contact sheets are 8×10 glossy sheets with thirty-seven small pictures on them.)

After the photographer sends you the contact sheets, about a week after the session, examine each picture with a magnifying glass and select two or three pictures that you think are the best.

The photographer then has those enlarged to 8×10 prints. All this is included in the up-front price of $125.

Don't have the photographer make duplicate glossies; it will be much too costly. Just take the one photo you've decided to send to agents and have it mass duplicated. You won't need the photographer's negative. Look in the *Yellow Pages* under "photo duplicating." The cost for duplicating glossies is usually less than twenty dollars for twenty-five prints, less than thirty dollars for fifty prints, and less than forty dollars for one hundred copies. The only other charge is for the 8×10 negative (which you get to keep) and it will cost about seven dollars. There are different paper qualities to choose from, but most agents prefer glossy prints. It is a good idea to have your name printed on each copy for a small additional charge.

While you are looking for an agent to represent you, don't have composites made up. A composite is a sheet of paper with one picture of you on the front and three, four, or five on the back. Composites are sometimes two or more pages long, sometimes in color, and can be very elaborate—and, at this stage, very much a waste of money. When you do get an agent, he or she (and you) will most likely want composites printed that include the agent's logo, address, and telephone number. No sense doing the job twice. Wait until you get an agent, then talk to him or her about composite requirements. Composites seem to be preferred almost everywhere over glossies, except in New York (see The Composite).

Now, before proceeding any further, don't have any pictures taken or pay anybody for a roll of film until you make certain you avoid the following very common mistakes.

While I was working on this book, my West Coast commercial agent gave me those ninety-five re-

jects sent to him each week that normally end up in the circular file. I put these photos in categories and came up with a number of common mistakes. These drawings represent photos that were actually submitted. Hard to believe . . .

PHOTOGRAPHS NOT TO SEND TO AN AGENT

Watch television for an evening. How many men do you see in commercials who need a shave, have a beard, or wear their hair long? How many women do you see with their hair in corn rows, bleached white, or with a purple tuft? Not too many. Right or wrong, a mold has been set for the commercial actor. If you fit into that mold, you increase your chances of finding an agent and finding work. Shave the beard, cut and comb the hair, *then* have your pictures taken. *No matter how attractive you feel your hair is, if it doesn't fit into the mold, you lessen your chances of finding work.*

Double-check the last time your photographer did a session. It may have been during the war. The Big One. Hats can be attractive in ads for Bloomingdale's, but an agent will want to see if you have hair, a white streak, a bald spot. Don't wear one.

These pictures went out of style a long time ago.

Is there really any difference between one photographer and another?

There sure is—not only in the photographer and his talent, but simply in the fact that you may or may not feel comfortable with him. Just as in real life, there are some people you feel at ease with and some you don't. Your relationship and feelings about the person taking your picture are as important as whether he knows how to focus his camera. It doesn't matter if he is technically the best in the world or if he has photographed all the greatest movie stars. If you feel uneasy, it will show.

The photos on the preceding two pages demonstrate this fact perfectly clearly. Suzy, my wife, had her first head shot (the one on the left) done by a professional photographer I'd used many times before. He always did a great job with my pictures, so I assumed that hers would also be great. Technically, he took a pretty good picture, but Suzy felt rushed and uncomfortable with him. The picture shows how uncomfortable she felt. She then searched for and found a photographer whom she felt very much at ease with and had her head shot redone. (The photo on the right.) What a difference! Even though the two pictures were taken only a few months apart, the actress on the right got an agent—the one on the left didn't have a chance.

What are the main differences between the two preceding pictures?

LEFT PHOTO	RIGHT PHOTO
• Tense, forced smile	• Relaxed, natural smile
• Background too sharp and orderly	• Background out of focus and fuzzy
• Contrast too high	• Contrast soft—shows shadings
• No highlight on hair for depth	• Hair has shadings and texture
• Shot in bright sun— eyes are squinting	• Shot in shade with reflected light on face
• Turtleneck makes subject look closed up	• Open plaid shirt looks casual
• Dull and lifeless	• High energy

The real smile doesn't happen when the photographer says "smile." Take your time. It starts in the heart, goes to the eyes, and ends up at the mouth. Not the other way around . . .

It's helpful to keep the atmosphere with the photographer on the light side so that your smile will come out of a natural giggle or laugh. Try talking to the photographer and stay animated. Don't just turn it on when you're supposed to.

What to wear when you have your picture taken:

• Dress conservatively—simple and wholesome. Don't dress seasonally or too fashionably. Don't wear white or black clothes.

• Don't wear a hat, jewelry, or any article of clothing unusual enough to draw attention away from your face. Men should never wear earrings.

• Women should wear light street makeup. Apply a little cover-up makeup if there are dark circles under your eyes.

• Don't wear glasses when having your picture taken. If you wear glasses, seriously consider getting contact lenses.

Now, let's review what your 8 × 10 glossy head shot should look like:

- Submit an 8 × 10 glossy picture. Your eyes should be in perfect focus.
- Always smile and show your teeth. Practice at home in the mirror.
- Make sure you are looking directly into the lens of the camera.
- Don't have yourself photographed in activity. Your pose should be relaxed.
- Use a head shot only, photographed against a simple background. Your hair and/or face shouldn't blend into the background.
- Don't use a photo that has too much contrast. Even black-and-white photos should have gray shading depicting skin tones.
- Make sure the picture you send is representative of you and how you look now. Stay away from the picture that everyone says is "sooo flattering." (That means it doesn't look like you at all.)
- Print your name and telephone number on the back of each picture.

THE RÉSUMÉ

In the same way that a good, clear, easy-to-look-at photograph is vital to attracting an agent, a good, clear, easy-to-look-at résumé is also important.

Now, before taking a look at what a résumé should be, take a good look at what it definitely should not be.

It's difficult to believe that anyone would submit a résumé that looked like this, but it does happen. The example above is almost identical to one sent to my Los Angeles agent.

No matter how much or how little experience you have, you can create a résumé that looks professional, is truthful, to the point, and easy to read. First, eliminate the irrelevancies, then categorize the important points, and you will have an impressive résumé.

Even with Arlene's résumé and list of questionable credits, a lot can be done to make it more acceptable. Let's try . . .

ARLENE ANYBODY
40-1/2 Lucky Lane
Los Angeles, California 90000
days—(151)555-1234
evenings—(151)555-1879

Height: 5'3"   Date of Birth: 4/1/61
Weight: 118 lbs.   Hair: Blond   Eyes: Hazel

FILM
MARITAL MADNESS   extra   Rank Film, Inc.

STAGE
AH, WILDERNESS!   Muriel   Podlunch Players
STAGE DOOR   Kaye (understudy)   Podlunch Players
ALL MY SONS   Ann   LAHS
DEEP ARE THE ROOTS   Genevra   LAHS
THIEVES' CARNIVAL   Juliette   LAHS
ROMEO AND JULIET   Juliet   LAHS
                                        (Best Actress Award)

MODELING
L.A. Modeling Agency   various engagements

TRAINING
Podlunch Players (under the direction of Laurence Podlunch)

SPECIAL ABILITIES
Dance (Jazz, Modern, Ballet, Tap, Disco)
Gymnastics

Congratulations, Arlene! That's a great-looking résumé.

WHAT A RÉSUMÉ SHOULD BE

- Have it typewritten, with no typographical errors or misspellings. *Everybody* knows *somebody* who can type.
- For category headings and your name use press-on letters which can be found at stationery stores. (Practice using the letters a few times to get the hang of the technique.)
- Your résumé should be one page in length.
- Use only the name you want to be known by. If you want to use a nickname, then include only that name. Try not to confuse the agent. ("Do I call you 'Snookie' or 'Arlene'?")
- Make sure you have a current telephone number (or numbers) where you can be reached both day and night.
- Leave out unnecessary information. Marital status and astrological signs are no-nos. It is best to omit your measurements. They are important for modeling, but not for commercial work.
- List the information on your résumé by categories. Start with experience, then on to training, then any special abilities you might have.
- Tell the truth. Include your real height, weight, and so on. If you don't wish to include your age, you may want to give a realistic age range. A birth date is a good idea, but don't fib. You'll get caught.
- Make sure your résumé is absolutely perfect. If it's less than that, you're wasting time, effort, and money.

There is the classic story of a young actor who felt his theatrical résumé didn't include enough impressive credits, so he invented a few. One of the credits he added was that he had appeared on a long-canceled television show shot on location in New York. Since he was based in California, he thought he was safe. When he went in to read for a new television show, the producer looked at his résumé,

suddenly developed a curious, then angry look on his face, and finally told him to leave.

You guessed it. The producer of this show produced the show in New York.

As I was glancing through the reject photos and résumés sent to my agent in California, one résumé in particular caught my eye. The young man was only twenty-two years old, yet he had listed a total of fifty-seven adult roles he had played onstage. If he'd started performing these roles at age eighteen, that's about fourteen shows a year! If you've been involved in fifty-seven plays then list them. If you've done fifty-seven scenes in acting class, then say they were scenes or don't list them on your résumé. Don't lie.

If you have some stage experience, but no film or TV credits, a résumé can help casting people, directors, producers, and clients remember you. It can also give you something to talk about. Even if you have no experience at all but have taken some acting classes, a résumé can be an icebreaker during an interview.

If you have no experience or credits, then it is best not to include a résumé when looking for an agent (or later during commercial calls). It is important to make yourself look as good as possible. Handing someone a blank résumé with your name on it isn't a good thing to do.

So, if you don't have any experience, don't worry. Many actors, those just starting and others already established, don't carry résumés. (In New York, it's much more common to see résumés than in Los Angeles.) The basic rule of thumb is this: If a résumé can help you, then include one. If not, leave it out.

Later, when you're working, you may choose to attach a résumé to your composite, but don't list the commercials you've done. You may be proud of each and every job, but listing them can only hurt you. To indicate the work you've done commercially on your résumé, merely say something like this:

> One or more commercials for each
> of the following advertising agencies:
> DFS—Dorland, Worldwide
> Ogilvy & Mather
> D'Arcy MacManus & Masius
> Leo Burnett

There are two reasons you shouldn't list your commercial credits by name on your résumé.

First, if I listed a commercial that I had done for Miller Beer and then went to audition for a Bud Light spot, I probably wouldn't be considered for the job. This would be true even if the first beer spot had been released two or three years before. Advertisers are funny that way.

Second, if, to look impressive, I listed one thousand commercials I've done over the years, the advertiser might feel I was "overexposed." This is an advertising phrase that means an actor may have too many commercials on the air and be too recognizable to the public, and would draw attention away from their product.

*Okay, now you've got
your 8 × 10 glossy and a
great-looking résumé,
and you're almost ready
to tackle the agent!*

*But before we make
that big step, let's take a
look at a few important
items that you might
have questions about.*

THE ANSWERING SERVICE

Every actor has two choices: Stay at home next to the telephone or use some kind of telephone answering service.

There are basically three kinds of answering services: the machine, the pickup service, and the central message exchange. Before choosing one that is right for you, take a look at the good and bad points of each.

I've had each of the above services at one time or another. I even rented a machine from the telephone company for two years before you could buy them. I have a recording machine now that I've had for five years and it still works fine. During those five years, I've moved a couple of times and all I've had to do was unplug the machine and take it with me. If I'd had a pickup service, I would have paid separate installation fees plus monthly charges. The machine is by far the cheapest way to go.

THE MACHINE

You can purchase this device almost anywhere. The cost ranges from under one hundred dollars to ten times that amount. Most machines you can install yourself in just a few minutes. When you're not at home and someone calls you, your machine answers the call and asks the caller to leave a message. It then records that message for you to hear when you return.

Advantages

• Once you buy your machine, there are no other costs.

• You can make your recorded message as clever as you want to. (This is great if you do impersonations, want background music in your message, and so forth.)

• Calls can be screened while you're at home and you can decide if you want to talk to the caller.

• For more money, you can have a machine that will page you on a beeper to let you know you have a call. Or, some machines come with a phone-in message retrieval system. You call your number and you can hear all the messages left on your machine.

Disadvantages

• Some people dislike talking to machines.

• If your mom calls long distance and you're not home, she loses her quarter.

THE PICKUP SERVICE

With this service your telephone number is connected to a switchboard at another location. When your phone rings, it rings at the switchboard, too. After a prescribed number of rings, a switchboard operator answers the call and takes a message.

Advantages

• There's a nice, personal touch when a human being asks for messages. (Unfortunately, sometimes the person asking for messages is less than nice and personal.)
• The switchboard operator can tell the caller where you are and when you are expected to return.
• If you are away from home, you can call the service and change messages.
• Some services have an electronic beeper you carry with you. If they have a message for you, they beep so that you can call them.
• You can leave specific messages for specific callers.
• You can use your service for reminder or wake-up calls.

Disadvantages

• Sometimes answering-service people are rude to you and your callers. Services are usually understaffed and the operators frequently put people on hold.
• There is an installation fee payable to the phone company and a monthly charge for the service.
• Probably the biggest complaint about pickup services is that they sometimes don't pick up.

THE CENTRAL MESSAGE EXCHANGE

This is a separate telephone number where people can call and leave a message for you.

Advantages

- There is no installation fee and the cost per month is much lower than for the pickup service.
- It's great if you're only going to be in town for a short time. I use one when I work in New York.
- You can give your personal telephone number to selected people and the exchange number to everyone else. This way you can screen calls and not be bothered at home.
- Most of the other advantages of the pickup service apply here as well.

Disadvantages

- These services handle a lot of messages. Yours may get lost or confused.
- You have to remember two different telephone numbers.
- There are the same problems as with the pickup service.

THE PUBLICATIONS

There are quite a few magazines, periodicals, trade journals, newspapers, and handbooks published for those who are serious about acting in television commercials. Many of these are very regional, so make sure the ones you buy apply to your geographical area. It would take an entire book to list every publication that has to do with show business, so I have selected just a few as representative. Again, don't rush out and subscribe to any until you find one that really interests you. To help you choose, a brief description is included with each one listed.

I read as many of these publications as I can. Many of them have interviews or bits of information about casting directors, directors, agency people. If you can keep a file on these people, you may find it invaluable in the future. If you read an article about a director and then have an interview or audition with him or her, you'll have a great deal more to talk about than the weather.

• *Back Stage* Back Stage Publications, Inc., 330 West 42nd Street, 16th floor, New York, NY 10036. Weekly newspaper/$35 per year. Good coverage of current information concerning commercial production in all parts of the country. Each section is divided into geographical areas. Interesting and informative.

• *Daily Variety* 1400 North Cahuenga Boulevard, Hollywood, CA 90027. M–F daily newspaper/$80 per year. Deals with the entertainment industry throughout the country. Occasionally has lists of actors doing commercials. Has a few advertisements for commercial acting classes in the Los Angeles area. Good industry information, but not directed toward the commercial actor.

• *Drama-Logue* P.O. Box 38771, Los Angeles, CA 90038–0771. Weekly/$36 per year. Stage, TV, film, industrial film casting news mostly for the Los Angeles area. Lists many commercial acting classes, dialect classes, cold-reading classes, photographers. Has interviews with casting directors, directors, actors. Geared toward the Los Angeles actor who does it all.

• *Geographic Casting Guide* Bons-Art Enterprises, P.O. Box 480276, Los Angeles, CA 90048. Quarterly/$4.50 per copy. Separate guides for the Los Angeles and New York areas. The best bet for a current list of all agents, casting directors, advertising agencies, film studios, TV stations, and union theatre producers. Even has a zip code map. Monthly updates of information are also available.

• *Hollywood Reporter* P.O. Box 1431, Hollywood, CA 90078. Daily/$89 per year. Geared to the Los Angeles area. Basically the same as *Daily Variety*. Good industry news, but not directed to the commercial actor.

• *LA 411* LA 411 Publishing, Inc., Raleigh Studios, Suite 122, Los Angeles, CA 90004. Yearly/$30. Published for the Los Angeles area, this is a production guide, not a guide for actors. A complete reference guide for the film, TV, and commercial production industry. Lists agents, ad agencies, production houses, directors, casting directors, studios, and unions, and everything from airline telephone numbers to national holidays. The New York counterpart is called *The Madison Avenue Handbook*, and in the Dallas area—*Dallas Shoot*.

• *New York Casting & Survival Guide* Peter Glenn

"It is always foolish to give advice. To give good advice is absolutely fatal."
Oscar Wilde

Publications, 17 East 48th Street, New York, NY 10017. Yearly/$13.85. A lot like *LA 411*, but geared to actors. If you're in the New York area, this is quite a handy book. Includes lists of casting directors and classes. Has street, subway, and city maps. Also includes a datebook and an employment record log for auditions and jobs.

• *Pacific Coast Studio Directory* 6313 Yucca Street, Hollywood, CA 90028. Quarterly/$7 per copy. All addresses and telephone numbers of anything related to the industry. Though it focuses mostly on the Los Angeles area, it also has listings for many other parts of the country.

• *Screen Actors News* SAG, 7750 Sunset Boulevard, Hollywood, CA 90046. Semimonthly/$7 per year. A cheaper version of the *Screen Actor Magazine* that SAG used to publish. Has monthly SAG union information and news.

In Appendix B, you'll find a list of all the commercial agents in the United States who are franchised by SAG and AFTRA. This includes the most current information available at printing time. Unfortunately, these names, addresses, and telephone numbers do have a habit of changing. I would suggest that you get the most up-to-date list possible by doing exactly what I did. Call or write SAG. I've also included each of the union chapter offices throughout the United States. They'll be happy to send you a current list (for a very modest fee) if you ask. Keep in mind that the unions are there to help you. Smile at them and they'll smile back.

You may also want to get a general-information magazine or newspaper. I suggest that you get a copy of some that are available in your area and *that service your area, and read them before subscribing. It does cost money!*

THE SCHOOLS

Any commercial actor, whether beginning or experienced, can learn more about the industry and craft. No matter how bright or successful an actor may be, there are always areas that can be improved upon and developed.

One way to learn more about this business, *especially* for the beginner just starting a career, is to attend a class that specifically teaches how to act in commercials.

There are many classes, schools, seminars (and even a correspondence course or two) devoted to acting in commercials. Some are legitimate, many are not. Before you pay to attend a class, make sure that it is a bona fide school that is more interested in you than your billfold. In the Los Angeles area, such schools are now being accredited by the state to ensure their validity and effectiveness. If you have *any* questions about the reputation of a school or class, call the Better Business Bureau in your area or call the state attorney general's office and ask for the Consumer Fraud Division, to see if they have received any complaints.

Should you decide to take a class in commercial acting, use the following guidelines. They will help you in your choice of a reputable school:

37

• Stay away from schools that advertise "all types of acting training." You need special classes in commercial acting.

• Beware of people who tell you that they can "get you into commercials." They can't. It doesn't happen that way.

• Don't be fooled by a fancy letter in the mail from a great-sounding school saying that you were "seen" somewhere, or your picture was "seen," and you have a great future in commercials. This may involve a "small fee" for a test of some kind (which will come out *very* positive), and then another "small fee" for consultation—and so on until you're broke.

• Don't go to a school that says you'll receive a diploma or letter of recommendation upon graduation which will guarantee you work. It will look nice on your wall, but you and your mom will be the only people who'll ever look at it. A reputable casting agent will laugh if you tell him or her that you should be considered for work because you have a diploma from a commercial acting school.

• Don't enroll in a school that offers a film or videotape of you appearing in various mock commercials. It's useless, expensive, and no one will ever see it.

There are several legitimate (and relatively inexpensive) classes, schools, and seminars you can take that will help you specifically in commercial acting. Many are taught through colleges and universities. Some are also conducted by reputable casting agencies and licensed by the state. This is a fantastic opportunity to learn from the people who really know the business, and it is a great way to meet the casting people and have them see you in action.

Rather than recommending specific schools or classes in each part of the country, I'll list some guidelines for finding the best classes available.

• Look in the trade papers and magazines for advertised classes (see The Publications). Call each one. Find out who teaches the classes and what qualifications they have. Find out what the classes cover, when they meet, how much they cost, how much on-camera training you get, the number of students in each class (the smaller the better), and whether franchised agents looking for new clients will be attending any class sessions. Also find out if guest speakers in the business are invited to lecture. Be sure to write down all the information.

• Call a few casting agencies and agents, tell them you're new in the business, and ask if they can recommend a particular class. Keep a list of the people you called and which class they recommended.

• Compare the lists you have in order to make a knowledgeable decision about which class might be best for your needs.

> *I personally feel that the right commercial acting class can be a genuine shortcut into the business. Everything I found out took me years to discover, and I made a lot of mistakes that could have been avoided if I'd taken a good class in the beginning. I'd also suggest, all other things being equal, that you take a class given by a reputable casting director. You'll get to know him or her, your work will be seen, and you might have an inroad to a commercial interview.*

"Show business is two percent show and ninety-eight percent business." An actor

THE UNIONS

There are two unions that on-camera actors in commercials need to be aware of: SAG and AFTRA. Basically it works like this:

• If you are an actor who is employed as on-camera talent for a commercial in a *filmed* medium, you must belong to the Screen Actors Guild (SAG).

• If you are an actor who is employed as on-camera talent for a *videotaped* commercial, then the American Federation of Television and Radio Artists (AFTRA) should be your union.

Since many commercials are filmed and many are videotaped, most actors who do commercials belong to both unions. (For a complete list of the specific chapters and their addresses, see Appendix B.)

Why are there unions?

Before any of the craft unions were formed, performers would be paid (or not paid) according to the whims of management. The amount of money paid to actors doing similar work could vary tremendously. Under union guidelines and agreed-upon contracts with the various employers, there are now standard fees paid for specific working situations. In order to employ the best talent available, management (everyone from the production company to the client and ad agency) signs very exact contracts with the unions.

Unions are set up to protect the rights of their members. They establish certain requirements for membership and offer medical and pension benefits.

Do I have to join the union to work as a principal performer?

The answer is yes if you are working for a SAG or AFTRA signatory. Many smaller advertising agencies in some of the smaller cities do nonunion television ads, and for these you need not be a union member. However, you may be paid less than union scale.

You do not need to be a union member to work at your first union job.

SCREEN ACTORS GUILD
How do I join?

In order to protect the members of SAG, the union has made it difficult to join. To be accepted you must

first audition for a commercial and get the job. Then the production company or the casting director has to request a Taft-Hartley waiver so that you can work as a nonguild member. They must also justify why they cast you and not a guild member. Once you receive the waiver by letter, you must start the job within two weeks, and then you're eligible to join the union, for a membership fee. If, however, you join a sister union such as AFTRA first, you may then join SAG at a reduced rate.

The problem is: It's difficult to get a job if you're not in the union, and almost impossible to get in the union without having a job.

Is there some other way?

Yes, there is a way around the SAG membership rule. The union states that if you have been a member of another craft union for one year and have proof that you've had a principal role as a performer at least once, you are eligible for SAG membership. The other unions are SEG (Screen Extras Guild), AEA (Actors Equity Association), AGVA (American Guild of Variety Artists), AGMA (American Guild of Musical Artists), and, most important, AFTRA.

AMERICAN FEDERATION OF TELEVISION AND RADIO ARTISTS

How do I join?

Easy. Just go to the local AFTRA chapter and pay.

More money?

Unfortunately, yes. AFTRA and SAG charge $650.00 to become members.

Semiannual dues for SAG begin at $37.50; AFTRA at $32.50. The amount you pay in dues is determined by how much money you earned through that particular union the previous year.

Okay, now you've got your pictures done, your résumé finished, and you're filled with knowledge about answering services, publications and trade papers, schools, and the unions. Let's take the next big step: getting an agent.

THE AGENT

People sometimes have a rather distorted image of the commercial agent.

Some people see the agent one way . . .

. . . while other people see him another way.

What is an agent?

Agents are businesspeople trying to eke out their living much the same as we are. They are usually honest, hardworking people who are carefully scrutinized and licensed by SAG and AFTRA, the on-camera actor's two governing unions. Their function for the commercial actor is to solicit job interviews and to negotiate any unusual terms not spelled out in established union contracts.

Do I really need an agent?

Yes. For the commercial actor, an agent is not only desirable but an absolute necessity. The producers of commercials employ casting agencies to locate actors and actresses who might be right for a particular com-

mercial. Casting agencies then call agents for suggestions and the agents submit their clients. The casting people will select some, reject others, and come up with a list of actors from a number of different agents. Those people are assigned a particular day and time for an audition. The agent is a middleman, but a vital one. It would be impossible for every actor to call every casting agency every day to find out if there are any jobs coming up and if they might be right for a part. Usually casting agencies won't take the time even to meet an actor unless he or she has representation.

How do I find an agent?

There are three ways actors find agents. One way is to have a friend already in the business who can get you an interview with his or her agent. The second way is to have an agent see your work. Many legitimate commercial acting classes include an "agents' night" as one of the last classes. The other way is to go about the process the same way most of us did who are now in the business.

What way is that?

Appendix B of this book has a current list of names, addresses, and telephone numbers of all commercial agents franchised by SAG and AFTRA. While it is true that the majority of agents (and advertising agencies) are in New York and Los Angeles, there are agents all over the country.

I suggest selecting up to five agents from this list every few days and sending them your 8×10 glossy and résumé with a typed, personalized, to-the-point note informing the agent that you are "seeking representation" in the commercial area. Avoid writing notes that are too clever or too cute. These are business people and you are looking for work, not a pen pal.

Here is a good approach:

To:
Alvin Starmaker
Starmaker Unlimited
470 S. San Vincent
Los Angeles, California 90000

From:
Arlene Anybody
40-1/2 Lucky Lane
Los Angeles, California 90000
(151) 555-1234 days
(151) 555-1879 evenings

Mr. Starmaker:

I am seeking representation in the
commercial area. Attached is a current
resume and photograph for your consideration.
I will be calling your office in a day or
so to hopefully meet with you personally.

Thank you for your time:

Arlene Anybody

Arlene Anybody

After you mail the packets with your note, photo, and résumé to the selected agents, be sure to check off which agents they were sent to and on which dates they were sent. Mail your material in a large manila envelope with cardboard for support so nothing arrives folded, spindled, or mutilated. Don't start at the top of the list and send your mailers alphabetically. Abrams-Rubaloff & Lawrence gets a lot more mail than the Bob Yanez Talent Agency.

Follow up your mailer with a pleasant telephone call about two days after you think it has been received. Don't wait for them to contact you. They probably won't. The best times to call are between 10:00 A.M. and 2:00 P.M., Monday through Thursday. Afternoons and Fridays are the busiest times for agents.

Your telephone call will usually be handled by a secretary. Your approach should be something like this:

The conversation will most likely end up one of three ways: They will hang up, tell you to call back, or ask you to set up an appointment.

Number One

If they hang up, cross them off your list and focus negative attention on them for five minutes.

Number Two

If they suggest you call back, log the information for a future call.

Number Three

If they ask you to set up an appointment, your foot's in the door!

MEETING THE PROSPECTIVE AGENT

The agent is meeting you because he saw something in your photograph and/or résumé that made him think you might make him some money. Remember this! Also remember that if he signs you to his client list, he is doing so for the same reason.

What should I talk about during the interview?

Be warm and friendly and as relaxed as possible. Remember there is nothing an agent would like better than to find someone that might make him some money. He may ask about some item on your résumé or he may ask you to read some commercial copy. Usually, however, he will ask the question most often asked during an interview: "Can you tell me a little about yourself?"

Here's what not *to do:*

John Wayne's advice to a young actor: "Talk low, talk slow, and don't say too much."

The idea is not to see how much information you can squeeze into an interview, but to find an area that might be of common interest and expand on it. How much you say during an interview isn't half as important as what you say and how excited you are about saying it. Plain information is boring. If you can find any topic your listener can relate to on a personal level, and it's an area you like to talk about or have some knowledge of, then you're both much more relaxed and at ease.

> *I have about ten topics I enjoy talking about that usually get my listener involved. My favorite subject is teaching. For quite a few years I acted professionally and taught at the same time. Teaching theatre has always been a great joy for me. Well, I discovered that almost everyone has had something to do with teaching. Either they taught during their spare time in a seminar class, or their mother or sister teaches school, or whatever. All of a sudden, "Tell me a little about yourself" becomes a conversation instead of a monologue. If you can get the listener (or the agent, in this case) to do more than listen, you're both going to have a pretty good time during the interview.*
>
> *On one commercial audition, I mentioned to a director that I taught school. It turned out he had taught, too, and was quite interested in the fact that I had stayed with teaching even though it wasn't financially necessary. We spent most of the interview talking about the need for more people in specific professions doing some practical-application teaching. To make a long story short, he ended up coming out to my school during his free time to guest lecture about film making, he gave one of my students a job, and hired me seven times that year for commercials.*
>
> *In another situation, during an audition for a part in a popular television series I discovered that the producer and I were alumni of the same college and had also been members of the same fraternity. Needless to say, that's where the conversation stayed. I ended up doing three episodes of that show.*

Now, if you were never a teacher or didn't belong to a fraternity, try to find something you both have in common. Look around. If you see that there are magazines on hang-gliding or sailing or backpacking in the waiting room, try to steer the conversation in that direction. "I

"The desire to succeed is nothing. Anybody who has ever dreamed has had a desire to succeed. The difference is someone who takes his raw talent and works his ass off." An anonymous agent

noticed that you have a lot of hang-gliding magazines in the lobby. Do you really hang-glide?'' You may find that the agent feels at ease, does a lot of the talking, and, after you leave, has a very positive feeling toward you.

Oh, one more reminder: Tell the truth.

How should I look for my interview?

It's very important to look as much like your photograph as possible. Don't grow a beard or mustache or dye your hair after your photo session. If you have additional pictures of yourself that are good, take them in too.

What should I wear?

Wear clothes you look good in and feel comfortable in. Watch television commercials for a day and see what

the actors you'll be competing with are wearing. A simple, wholesome image will put you in the best light with an agent. Agents look at prospective clients the same way Procter & Gamble looks at prospective actors for their ads.

Aren't some agents better than others?

Yes. And no. Don't judge an agency by its size or by what you've heard. The biggest may not necessarily be the best. An agent can be great for one actor who happens to be working a lot and terrible for another actor who is on the unemployment line. If the agency's been in business for a while and is franchised by the unions, it must be making money from booking at least some of its actors in jobs.

How much do agents get paid?

Nothing—until you work. An agent who represents you or sends you on a commercial call receives no

money unless you get the job. When you do work, the agent gets ten percent of your gross paycheck. No more. No less. (For more specific details, see The Money.) Remember that an agent makes money only if you make money. If someone tells you otherwise, he's a crook!

Can I have more than one agent represent me?

Yes. And no. In Los Angeles, you may have only one commercial agent. In New York, actors can free lance with more than one agent representing them. The exclusivity rule varies depending on the geographic area.

I find it easier to keep records straight and watch for conflicts (see The Money), if I have only one agent on each coast. This is a matter of personal preference.

How often should I contact my agent?

Once a week if you haven't heard from him. Remind him in a positive way that you're around. If you happen to be performing in a play, make sure he's the first to know. Let him know that you're working hard to further your career. If you're going out of town for a few days, call and tell him. Try to find a reason to call him so you'll stay on his mind. Find out when his birthday is and drop him a card. Drop off a pumpkin on Halloween.

Don't make the mistake of calling and saying, "What have you done for me this week?" Keep it on the positive side.

Congratulations! Your search for the right agent has proven to be profitable. You are now ready to move on to the next section in your search for a career in commercials—After the Agent. Good luck.

AFTER THE AGENT

The Composite

The Preparation and the Waiting

The Audition

The Job

The Money

THE COMPOSITE

What's a composite?

A composite is a printed, two-sided sheet of four to six photographs, which serves as an actor's 8½ × 11 calling card when he or she goes on a commercial audition. See the examples on pages 68–71.

I need more pictures taken? Sounds like I have to spend more money. How come?

Sorry, you do have to spend a little more, but this will save you money in the long run—honest.

Leaving a composite at an audition is a lot less expensive than leaving a glossy. Glossies, even mass printed, cost a minimum of forty cents apiece (sometimes up to and over two dollars). Composites cost about one hundred and twenty-five dollars per five hundred, or about twenty-five cents apiece.

More important, a composite is a better tool for you to use in getting work. A head shot, no matter how good it is, shows you with only one expression, location, set of clothes. A composite shows you in four to six different pictures.

The composite I describe in this section is typical of an acceptable composite in Los Angeles. However, all agents and agencies in various cities differ in their preference of composite size, texture, number of pictures, and so on. Most actors in New York use 8 × 10 glossies and don't carry composites. I have found that taking my composite rather than a glossy when I'm auditioning in Manhattan can be an advantage. Casting directors will automatically ask how long I'll be in town. It serves as a great conversation starter. Be sure to find out what is preferable in your geographic area before spending any money.

How do I get my composite done and what will it cost?

Your new agent can be a great help in this area. He undoubtedly will provide guidelines for you to follow as far as layout, using his logo, type size of the print, different poses he wants, clothes that seem best for your type, and so on.

Your agent may also suggest a photographer or two that he's used before. Your agent should not get a "cut" or a percentage from the photographer he sends you to. That's unethical.

If he doesn't have any suggestions and is pleased with your initial head shot, you may choose to go back to your original photographer. Whoever you use, shop around the same way you did for your head shot. And again: Before you pay anyone to take your pictures, make triple sure he's the right one. Take a good look at his portfolio.

His portfolio may give you some good ideas for your own composite. If you use a new photographer, make sure you take in your old pictures to point out what you don't like about them. A good photographer will see the problems right away.

The average fee for a photo session is about $225 to $275. The session will probably take three to four hours at four to six locations. The photographer will shoot six or so rolls of 36-exposure, 35mm. film, which he will have printed into contact sheets. You then select about six pictures, and they will be blown up to 8 × 10 glossies. All this is included in the initial price.

59

Your agent should help you select which pictures you want blown up. He's had more practice than you've had—and he's also *much* more objective than you (and your mom) are.

Your agent will then help you decide on the layout of your composite and select a print shop. Again, the cost is about $125 for five hundred copies.

Before you start, discuss with your agent and your photographer which categories you're best suited for and then bring the clothes that would be most appropriate. For instance, a thirty-year-old man could wear a suit and tie for a spokesman photo, an open shirt and sweater (and a child) for a daddy picture, and a construction hat and work clothes for a blue-collar type photo.

How do I know what "type" I am?

Finding your type can be a little harder than it sounds. It's much easier to have someone else categorize you than it is to do it yourself. Here's a list of some of the more common types used in commercials. Watch television for an evening, see if you can spot each of them, and

then visualize yourself in each of the roles. If you still have trouble deciding which ones fit you best, ask your agent for help. You may just open his eyes to the fact that you have more than one type.

COMMERCIAL TYPES

The Housewife	The Young Husband
The Young Mother	The Father
The Girl-Next-Door	The Guy-Next-Door
The Fast-Food Counter Girl	The Fast-Food Counter Guy
The Cosmetic Model	The Cosmetic Model
The Ditzy Blonde	The Lumberjack
The Wolf-Whistle Bombshell	The Handsome Man
The One-Calorie Girl	The Athlete
The Female Executive	The Male Executive
The Granny	The Granddad
The Character	The Character
The Spokeswoman	The Spokesman

How often do I need to have new pictures taken for my composite?

Obviously, whenever you look different from your pictures! It is absolutely essential that you look like your photographs. The minute you go from brunet to blond, or from 115 pounds to 135 pounds, get your composite redone.

Even if you don't change your weight or your hairstyle, you should get a new composite at least once a year. You may not think you look much different from your high-school graduation picture, but you do.

What guidelines should I follow for my composite?

• Follow the same guidelines you used for your initial head shot (see The Photograph).

• If you and your agent like the photograph you used to find your agent, then use it. It may be great for the front photo.

• No two pictures should have the same expression,

show the same clothing, or be in the same location. Each one should be a unique, terrific, energetic photo of you.

• Use head shots only. As a rule, full-figure shots are used for modeling.

If you happen to be a young mother, father, granny, or granddad type, you might want to include a child in one of the composite pictures. If you do, get a nice, agreeable one for an hour or so and make sure to have his or her *back* to the camera. There's an old rule of thumb for stage actors—never appear onstage with a child or an animal. If you do, no one's going to pay any attention to you! Don't upstage yourself.

• Traditionally, most photographs for a composite are taken outdoors. It tends to make the photo look candid. However, the sun can cause squint marks and a pinched-face look, so make sure there is plenty of shade. The best times to shoot pictures are early in the morning or the late afternoon when the sun is not as strong.

Now that I'm in my forties (early!), I prefer all pictures to be shot indoors. Indoor lighting is much easier to control. Even the head shot on the front of my composite (see page 68) was shot in a studio using an outdoorsy backdrop.

• Make sure your hair and clothes don't blend into the background. If you have dark hair, don't stand in front of a dark tree.

• If you want to use a shot of you in a tennis outfit with a racquet, make sure that you do play. (No fibbing—even in pictures). A shot of you smiling, holding a racquet, is much better than an action shot.

• Remember that your object is to look like the average American.

• Find out what the usual composite looks like in your geographic area and follow those guidelines exactly. Oversized pictures don't fit into casting books. Color costs a lot, but if no one else uses color, it's a waste. Concentrate on making your composite and each picture the best they can possibly be, not just on being different.

• Don't clutter up your composite with too many pictures. More than four on one side of a page is too many.

• Make sure your name and your agent's logo are on the front side and your name is also on the rear of the composite. Your agent may want you to include your height, weight, hair, and eye color.

• And, last: If you skipped ahead to this section without reading about the head shot, *never have a com-*

posite done before you get your agent! It's a waste of money.

Okay, I'm using my head shot for the front of the composite. What sort of pictures go on the back?

• **The Consumer:** Usually shot at a market, fast-food place, or restaurant. You are reacting to the taste, smell, size of a product. Incidentally, don't show the label of the product you're holding: that Pepsi bottle could shoot you down for a Coca-Cola spot. Clients are funny that way.

• **The Mommy/Daddy:** Usually shot at a park, school, playground, and so forth. Borrow a child if you don't own one (make sure you borrow a pleasant one). The focus of the photograph should be on you, not the child.

• **The Sports Enthusiast:** Pick a sport that you really do play and don't show too much activity. Rather

than a shot of you playing tennis, get a shot of you before or after you play. Remember, your face is the most
important thing in the picture. Oh . . . don't show too
much skin or hair on your chest. Procter & Gamble isn't
fond of that either.

• **The Businessman/Woman or Secretary:** Usually shot around an office building somewhere near
stairs, door, desk. Use a briefcase, papers, or a type-
writer for props. This could be a more serious shot, but
make sure you show energy.

Remember, it's not the terrific locations, clothes, or
attractive backgrounds that make great pictures for
your composite; it's *you*, your face, and the amount of
energy you project. Your composite is your calling card.
It can help you land a job—or it can lose you a job. It
should be the best combination of pictures that you can
possibly put together. Agents send out composites to
casting directors even before an actor is considered for
an audition, so a good composite can certainly get you
in the door. It will also stay in the files of people making
casting choices for other work, long after you've left the
audition.

How should I arrange my pictures on my composite?

This depends on the size of each photo after cropping. Here are a few suggestions, particularly for the Los Angeles market:

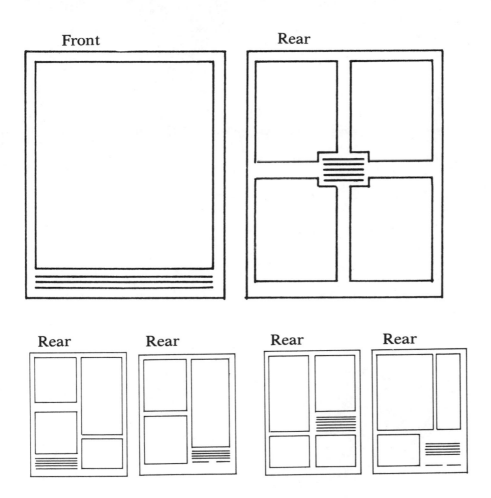

The following pages show the front and back of the composites my wife and I use for our Los Angeles commercial auditions. Their actual size is 8½ × 11 and they have three holes prepunched in them to fit into a casting director's book.

SQUIRE FRIDELL

SQUIRE FRIDELL

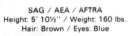

SAG / AEA / AFTRA
Height: 5' 10½'' / Weight: 160 lbs.
Hair: Brown / Eyes: Blue

SUZY FRIDELL
SAG / AFTRA

SUZY FRIDELL
SAG / AFTRA
Height: 5'2" / Weight: 104 lbs.
Hair: Brown / Eyes: Hazel

THE PREPARATION AND THE WAITING

Should I just wait for my agent to call me?

No! This is a very competitive business. If you hustle, you'll be more successful.

Get a list of all the casting people in your area (see The Publications). Call each of them and find out which ones are receptive to meeting new people. If you can arrange to meet with them in person to leave your head shot or composite and résumé, then do it. Those who aren't too excited about having a face-to-face meeting (these are busy people) will probably ask you to send in your picture. Some production houses and ad agencies have their own casting people, so don't overlook them. Every contact is a possible job.

Also, don't hesitate to study acting and acting for commercials. Study dance and pantomime, study voice and singing, study anything you like, but continue to grow. If you can get involved with a little theatre group, even to paint sets or take tickets, do it. You'll learn more about your craft and you'll meet people involved in the industry.

Here's a good tip given to me by a casting director: Instead of mailing your composite or photo and résumé in a 9 × 12 manila mailer, fold your picture and put it in a business envelope with a sheet of typing paper concealing the contents. Casting directors know what's in manila mailers and they tend to pile up in the office unopened for a while. Envelopes seem to get opened right away.

Watch television! While it's customary to go to the refrigerator when the commercials come on, pay attention to the TV set. Look at the people doing commercials and repeat their words right after them. Try to make the lines sound as real and convincing as you can. Take advantage of these free commercial acting classes. Another idea is to practice reading copy from newspaper and magazine ads.

If you play tennis, ride horseback, hang-glide, ride motorcycles, or ride skateboards, keep those skills alive. You never know when someone will be looking for a person to drop out of an airplane on a motorcycle pulling a horse on a skateboard while hitting an overhead smash shot.

A few years ago, I auditioned for an airline commercial, and they asked if I could ride a pogo stick. My heart skipped two beats; it finally paid off! I jumped on the pogo stick they had at the interview and did the entire audition hopping around the room. I got the job and immediately called my

mother and told her that all those years I spent on my pogo stick were worth the dents in the linoleum floor. (And she thought I was just scrambling my brains. It was research!)

I've also gotten commercials because I can ride a horse and a motorcycle, swim, sail, paddle a canoe, juggle eggs, play golf, ride a trotter, fly model airplanes, talk CB lingo, dribble a basketball, hop around in a gorilla suit, and hang from a wire seventy-five feet off the ground without losing my lunch. You never know.

Now that I'm going to make my living as a commercial actor, how soon can I quit my job?

Don't make that mistake. A lot of actors do and are sorry on the first of the month when the rent comes due. Most actors have other vocations to supplement their income. Some are secretaries, photographers, clerks, salespeople, teachers, parking attendants. Keep your job and see if you can make the hours flexible enough to squeeze in auditions. This way you'll have other income so you'll have the right attitude about the job you're auditioning for. As soon as it becomes a matter of life and death to get that commercial, you'll lose it. There's an old saying: "Nobody hires a hungry actor."

I continued to teach high school and college long after I didn't need it to earn a living. The salary wasn't important, but because I was working I felt I really didn't need the commercial or acting job. It made me more relaxed at auditions and a step ahead of the competition.

What about rejection?

Probably the most defeating thing every actor has to deal with is a huge amount of rejection. Rejection may come because you are an untried, unproved talent . . . or because you have been too successful and are overexposed. For every job you get, there will probably be countless ones that you did not get. And even after all those rejections, there is still no guarantee that you'll find work.

A salesperson has a hard job—competing with other salespeople to sell a product to a customer. As a salesperson, however, it's pretty easy to divorce yourself from the product. You can always rationalize your lack of sales on the inferiority of the product you sell. Actors, on the other hand, have only themselves as their product—their face, the shape of their nose, their hairline, their build, their voice. After a number of consecutive no's, actors tend to question their product.

Many people who go into acting have a very strong desire to perform in front of people or in front of a camera. These people sometimes have egos that are unfortunately as fragile as they are large. Keep this in mind as you examine acting as a career. It may not be the right one for you.

What about success?

Even if there is some degree of success, acting, whether it is onstage, in film, on TV, or in commercials, may not be the right choice for you. In this business the highs can be very high, but they are also short-lived. The lows, on the other hand, are very low and seem to last for a long time. The elation usually lasts about an hour after you discover that you got a job. You call your folks and your friends and tell them of your good fortune. But after your hour of highs, you'll be busy preparing for a long day's work. There's a wardrobe call, a script to memorize, and probably no sleep the night before. Then it hits you, that sinking, low feeling, usually on your way home from the work day. Where will your next job come from?

What can I do about all the stress that seems to be associated with this business?

First and foremost, make sure that you have another source of steady income. Even if you have incredible success and land that elusive first commercial on your first audition, keep your regular job until you're *sure* that you can continue to make your monthly payments.

> *I started making money as an actor during my third year of teaching high school in Southern California. The following year I was making more as an actor than as a teacher. Even though my acting income increased each succeeding year, I stayed with teaching full time for nine years—always thinking of teaching as my real vocation and acting as an avocation.*

Live within your income and don't make payments on anything except real estate. If you can't afford to buy a car, don't buy one on time. Wait until you can afford it and you'll save all that interest.

> *When I first started acting professionally, I had a good friend who began about the same time. After landing his first national commercial for NyQuil, he made a down payment on a great-looking Porsche Speedster he'd always wanted. Six months later he was walking. Don't buy a car on time.*

Stay away from trying to alter your mood with drink or drugs. It may work for a bit, but it's a quick road to an unsuccessful future. It also can make for a very short career.

Keep busy. Even if you happen to be the favorite nephew of a rich uncle who is paying all your bills, get active and stay as busy as you can. The busier you are, the less time you'll have to experience stress between those all-important phone calls. If you *ever* find yourself sitting at home staring at the telephone, you're both physically and mentally in the wrong place. Waiting for your career to develop is neither realistic nor healthy.

If you find a local theatre group to work with, by all means join them. There are very few cities and towns in this country that don't have at least one amateur group of thespians. Even if you're not acting onstage right away, you can paint sets, run lights, usher, or take tickets at the door. Not only will you make friends with people who may be able to guide you in your career, but you'll be adding to that résumé while you learn more and more about the business.

During my second year of teaching school in Southern California, I started working with a small theatre group called South Coast Repertory. I'd teach school all day, then run down to the theatre at night and take tickets, paint bathrooms and makeup rooms, stage manage, and act. One night a casting director from Los Angeles named Ramsay King came to see a production I was acting in. After the show he introduced himself and suggested that I get an agent and try to work professionally. With some assistance from him, I was able to get started on the right path. The four years that I spent at that theatre kept me busy at something I loved, taught me a great deal about my future profession, and proved to be the stepping stone to working professionally. I made friends at SCR that have been and will continue to be friends for a long, long time.

Another way to keep busy is to develop some sort of athletic program. Even if you're the sort who always came in last when forced to run laps in physical-education class, there *is* a sport for you. Millions of people find healthful enjoyment in jogging, aerobic exercise, racquetball, tennis, swimming, horseback riding, whatever. Not only will exercising take the edge off those stressful periods between telephone calls, but you'll get into great physical shape as well. You'll look good and you'll feel good.

Try to find a hobby that you'll enjoy. Join a club or a group and stay active with them. Learn to play piano or guitar. Learn to juggle. Any and all of these suggestions accomplish the same thing. You'll be active, you'll be busy, and you won't have time to worry about your lack of telephone calls.

My wife and I discovered a great place to take inexpensive classes (sometimes even free): our local community college. Our local college gives instruction in everything from art to clothing design. There are classes in child rearing, theatre, foreign languages, piano, voice, photography, dance, and even a class in stress management. The programs were developed for you, so take advantage of them.

In 1971, I did the most intelligent thing I've ever done to help my career (and my life): I started Transcendental Meditation, a simple relaxation technique done twice a day for twenty minutes that relieves stress and fatigue. It lowered my high blood pressure and gave me a stress-release valve I badly needed. Many people in high-stress occupations regularly practice TM. My wife found it helped her in dance (she was with the Nikolais Dance Theatre Company in New York for eight years). People like Ned Beatty, Steve Collins, Burt Reynolds, Clint Eastwood, Merv Griffin, Doug Henning, Joe Namath (and my wonderful illustrator, Barry Geller) all swear by its effectiveness. I still meditate twice a day. I learned long ago that the only thing that stops most actors from doing well in an audition is nervousness and stress. I want to do well in every audition.

78

THE AUDITION

ALIAS: THE INTERVIEW
THE CALL
THE READING

Sounds a little frightening, doesn't it? Well, don't be scared off. The more you know about the audition before you actually have that first reading, the more relaxed you'll be and the better you'll perform. The Audition chapter is a rather large one that is broken down into a number of areas. Follow each section carefully and soon you'll be on your way to the call-back and the job.

There are two items you should take the time to purchase at this point. Buy an appointment book. Be sure to keep an accurate record of every commercial audition, photo session, meeting with your agent, trip to the dentist, and so forth. If you are audited by the IRS (and many actors are), you'll need proof for deductions.

> *The first year I was audited, my records were terrible and I suffered because of it. The second year (and subsequent years) I did much better. Keep good records.*

The second thing you should buy is a little book to log information about anything and everything that might some day help you in this business. Write down the names of casting people you meet, the names of their secretaries, whether or not a particular casting director likes you to mention your agent's name during the audition, whatever. Jotting down your agent's birthday might not be a bad idea. Remember, this is a very competitive business. Anything that can give you an edge over other actors may mean the difference between working and not working.

THE PRELIMINARIES

When you finally do get that telephone call from your agent telling you that you've got an audition, there are five things you should write down:

1. Where the audition will be held
2. What time you are scheduled to read
3. The name of the casting director
4. Which commercial product you'll be reading for
5. A hint of the character and appropriate clothing to fit that character

• *Where the audition will be held:* Make sure you understand exactly where the audition is going to be. Ask for directions if you don't know the area. Ask about the easiest route, what the cross streets are, any landmarks in the area. Don't be afraid to ask. If you don't have a map of the area that shows streets and numbers of blocks, buy one. Figure out your route before you get on the bus, subway, or in your car.

• *What time you are scheduled to read:* Be on time! Nothing unnerves a casting director more than an actor late to an audition. Schedule plenty of travel time to arrive at the audition early, so you can relax and work on the script or copy.

• *The name of the casting director:* A lot of actors show up at interviews, sign in, sit down, and never acknowledge the casting director. If you're unsure whether the person behind the desk is, in fact, the casting director—introduce yourself and ask.

• *Which commercial product you'll be reading for:* This is a good time to mention conflicts. There is an enforceable rule that an actor cannot appear on-camera in more than one commercial in the same category for a specific period of time. If you've done a commercial for Toyota, you may not perform in any other automobile commercials as long as Toyota has you on hold (see The

Money). Be very careful! The penalties are incredibly steep: They can legally force you to pay for an entire recasting session and the shooting of another commercial. Don't just assume you are released from a commercial because they aren't playing it anymore. Ask your agent to check. Don't let him assume, either. He's not legally responsible; *you* are.

• *A hint of the character and appropriate clothing to fit that character:* Try to dress for the part as much as you can. If your agent fails to give you an idea of what the character is like, ask him. A spokesperson for IBM will certainly be dressed differently from a tennis player promoting Gatorade. Always ask your agent if you're in doubt about the acceptability of a particular garment. When you are given a general suggestion for what to wear, relate it to specific clothing that you own and ask your agent if your outfit will be appropriate for the call.

WHAT TO WEAR TO THE AUDITION

• Be aware of the different clothes the actors wear in different television commercials.

• Plaid shirts for men and women are a standard garment for commercials. Make sure you have a couple of them. The patterns should be bright and cheerful, but not too busy or loud, and always stay away from patterns with distinctly sharp parallel lines. They do funny things to the videotape. Long sleeves are better than short. Black and white are out.

• Unless specifically asked to, never bare your shoulders or wear suggestive or trendy clothes.

• Keep your gold chains, earrings, and other jewelry at home. Anything that draws attention away from you is out.

• It's always a good idea to bring along a change of clothing to change your look if necessary.

MAKEUP TIPS (FOR WOMEN *AND* MEN)

• Your fingernails should be of acceptable length for your sex, nicely trimmed, and clean. Many times during an audition, you'll be asked to hold up your hands. Your hands may be photographed handling their product. Women should wear clear or conservative polish colors.

• Women's lipstick should be conservative. Don't use gloss. If you have any doubts about the acceptability of a color, be sure to ask your agent.

"It's better to look good than to feel good." A makeup artist to an actor

• All women's makeup should fall into the category known as "light street makeup."

• Hair should be of an acceptable length. If your hair is colored, make sure it looks natural and that no roots show.

• Men should not have a beard line. It may be necessary to shave again midday if you have a call late in the day.

• Dark lines and shadows around the eyes and slight blemishes can be erased with a cover-up makeup, but be sure that it blends well with your skin. (Men can use it too!)

• Remember that makeup is designed to make you look *better*, not *different*.

BEFORE YOU LEAVE FOR THE AUDITION

Leave yourself plenty of time to get there so that you won't have to be concerned with the possibility of being late. Check to see that you have your head shot or composite and résumé with you. (Always have a spare.) Take the time to grab any props you may want to bring (more about this soon).

BEFORE YOU GET THERE

Some tips on things to do on your way to your audition:

• Be happy with your wardrobe, hair, and makeup. It's too late to change them, so be satisfied with your selections.

• You'll feel a little nervous; remember that everyone does. The nervous feeling is adrenaline, which is a good thing. The body releases adrenalin when it knows that it needs to do something special. Treasure that feeling.

• Be happy that you are going on an interview and be confident that you'll do the best possible job.

• Smile to yourself. It may become a habit.

• Use this time to make sure your vocal instrument works. If the first word you've said all day is your greeting to the casting director, something disastrous might happen. Vocal cords are muscles, so loosen them up.

I feel that a vocal warm-up is one of the most vital things to do before an audition. On your way to the call, pick out a speech, poem, tongue twister, or a song that you know the words to. Recite it and enunciate each syllable, vowel, and consonant. Stretch your tongue and cheeks and open your mouth as wide as you can. I like to practice the "Trouble in

River City" song from The Music Man *before an au-*
dition. It really gets my voice ready, loosens up my
face, and gets my energy level up. Other favorite
warm-up pieces are "Jabberwocky" by Lewis Carroll
and the nightmare sequence from Gilbert and Sul-
livan's Iolanthe.

Here are a few good exercises that will warm up
your vocal body parts.

For developing flexibility in the tip of the tongue:
Theophilus Thistle, the successful thistle sifter, sifting a
sieve full of unsifted thistles, thrust three-thousand thistles
through the thick of his thumb. Now if Theophilus Thistle,
the successful thistle sifter, in sifting a sieve full of unsifted
thistles, thrust three-thousand thistles through the thick of
his thumb, see that thou in sifting a sieve full of unsifted
thistles, thrust not three-thousand thistles through the
thick of thy thumb. Success to the successful thistle sifter.
(Fifteen seconds with no mistakes is excellent!)

To increase flexibility of the lips: *I bought a batch of*
baking powder and baked a batch of biscuits. I brought a
big basket of biscuits back to the bakery and baked a basket
of big biscuits. Then I took the big basket of biscuits and
the basket of big biscuits and mixed the big basket with the
basket of big biscuits that was next to the big basket and
put a bunch of biscuits from the baskets into a box. Then I
took the box of mixed biscuits and a biscuit mixer and the

biscuit basket and brought the basket of biscuits and the box of mixed biscuits and the biscuit mixer back to the bakery and opened up a can of sardines.

(Fifteen seconds with no mistakes is again excellent.)

Try this one from Gilbert and Sullivan's *Iolanthe* in one breath: *You're a regular wreck, with a crick in your neck, and no wonder you snore, for your head's on the floor, and you've needles and pins from your soles to your shins, and your flesh is a-creep for your left leg's asleep, and you've cramps in your toes, and a fly on your nose, and some fluff in your lung, and a feverish tongue, and a thirst that's intense, and a general sense that you haven't been sleeping in clover.*

Here's my favorite. It's "Jabberwocky" from Lewis Carroll. The words are ones that he made up from other words.

John Barrymore's stage debut found him forgetting his first line. He blurted out to his fellow actor: "I've blown up, old chap. Where do we go from here?"

> *'Twas brillig, and the slithy toves*
> *did gyre and gimble in the wabe.*
> *All mimsy were the boroughgroves*
> *And the mome raths outgrabe.*
>
> *"Beware the Jabberwock, my son;*
> *The jaws that bite, the claws that catch.*
> *Beware the Jub-Jub Bird,*
> *And shun the frumious Bandersnatch!"*
>
> *He took his vorpal sword in hand;*
> *Long time the manxome foe he sought.*
> *So rested he by the Tum Tum tree,*
> *and stood awhile in thought.*
>
> *And as in uffish thought he stood,*
> *The Jabberwock, with eyes of flame,*
> *Came whiffling through the tulgey wood*
> *And burbled as it came!*
>
> *One two! One two! And through and through*
> *the vorpal sword went "snicker snack."*
> *He left it dead, and with it's head*
> *He went galumphing back.*

"And hast thou slain the Jabberwock?
Come to my arms, my beamish boy!
Oh frabjous day! Calooh! Calay!"
He chortled in his joy.

'Twas brillig, and the slithy toves
Did gyre and gimble in the wabe.
All mimsy were the boroughgroves
And the mome raths outgrabe.

WHEN YOU ARRIVE

You've made it! You've come a long way to get this far and you should be proud of yourself. You're on time, you have your composite or glossy in hand, you've done your facial and vocal exercises, you look good, you feel good. Right now, there's no one who has a better chance than you do of landing that commercial. Now, take a couple of deep breaths, let out a sigh, relax your shoulders, stand up straight, smile, and open the door.

THE WAITING ROOM

Waiting rooms are usually small areas with not quite enough chairs for all the people who wish to occupy them. If there isn't a place to sit after you've signed in and received the copy, don't take it as a personal affront. Just wait until a chair is vacated. You may even prefer to stand. It keeps that energy up.

The number of actors you'll be competing with varies at each audition. Sometimes there will be only a few; other times there will be hundreds. Don't be unnerved by the number of actors in the room, who they may be, or what they may say. You're on the same call as they are and have just as much chance of getting that job as they do at this point. Also, don't be awed by anyone. The face you recognize from a million commercials may have an overexposure problem, and you may be a better

choice for the job. Just smile, be friendly, and be positive. Competition is stiff; actors can (and will) do funny things to one another at auditions. Don't let it affect you.

As you look around the waiting room, don't panic if you are the only short brunet in a room of six-foot blonds. Don't try to figure out the logic or the odds. Just be yourself and do your best. If you're not right for the job, at least you had an opportunity to audition and they might remember you for something else. You may also get the job because they were bored with six-foot blonds.

THE SIGN-IN SHEET

On the following page there is a copy of a SAG commercial-audition sign-in sheet. When you sign in, enter all the necessary information in a clear, legible hand. The sure sign of a beginner is one who has to look up his Social Security number, so make sure you memorize it.

The sign-in sheet serves a number of purposes. It lets the casting director know you're there, provides your Social Security number, the name of your agent, your actual call time, your time of arrival, and whether or not you are on a call-back. Occasionally, first-interview actors will be on the same call with those who are being called back for the job. It means nothing as far as your chances, so don't let it bother you. The union sign-in sheet is also important for the actor. Union rules stipulate that the actor can only be at the interview for one hour following the actual call time. After that, the actor must be paid for his or her time. Casting directors try to schedule actors at intervals so that there won't be a problem with overtime.

If there is a blatant overtime violation, I'd suggest doing what everyone else is doing. If no one seems to be signing out at overtime, then don't be the only one.

COMMERCIAL PLAYERS
1. Print your name.
2. Print agent's name.
3. Circle applicable interview

EXHIBIT E
SCREEN ACTORS GUILD
COMMERCIAL AUDITION REPORT FORM

AUDITION DATE _____

CASTING REP. _____ COMMERCIAL TITLE _____
ADVERTISER _____ PRODUCT _____ JOB # _____
ADV. AGENCY _____ CITY _____ PRODUCTION CO. _____

PLAYER'S NAME (PRINT)	SOCIAL SECURITY #	(PRINT) AGENT	PLAYER'S ACTUAL CALL	PLAYER'S TIME IN	PLAYER'S TIME OUT	PLAYER'S INITIALS	CIRCLE INTERVIEW #
							1st 2nd 3rd 4th
							1st 2nd 3rd 4th
							1st 2nd 3rd 4th
							1st 2nd 3rd 4th
							1st 2nd 3rd 4th
							1st 2nd 3rd 4th
							1st 2nd 3rd 4th
							1st 2nd 3rd 4th
							1st 2nd 3rd 4th
							1st 2nd 3rd 4th
							1st 2nd 3rd 4th
							1st 2nd 3rd 4th
							1st 2nd 3rd 4th
							1st 2nd 3rd 4th
							1st 2nd 3rd 4th
							1st 2nd 3rd 4th
							1st 2nd 3rd 4th
							1st 2nd 3rd 4th
							1st 2nd 3rd 4th
							1st 2nd 3rd 4th
							1st 2nd 3rd 4th
							1st 2nd 3rd 4th
							1st 2nd 3rd 4th

PRODUCER
1. Complete top half of form.
2. Sign your name.
3. Mail white copy to SAG on 1st and 15th of each month.
4. Designate person to whom correspondence concerning this form shall be sent _____

PRODUCER must provide players with cue cards or a mechanical prompting device at all on-camera filmed or video taped auditions.

SIGNATURE OF AUTHORIZED REPRESENTATIVE

If it's only a few minutes, it's probably best not to sign out late and risk not getting another interview from that casting director.

THE INFORMATION SHEET/ SIZE CARD

NAME _____ HOME PHONE _____

ADDRESS _____

AGENT_____ PHONE _____

SS# _____ AGE ____ BIRTH DATE_____

SUIT/DRESS _____ SHIRT/BLOUSE _____

SHOE_____ HAT_____ PANTS _____

BEING SEEN FOR _____

SPECIAL SKILLS_____

WORK PERMIT# _____ (CHILDREN)

EXP. DATE _____ (CHILDREN)

On some auditions you may find information sheets and/or size cards to fill out. Be truthful about everything. If you wear a size 12 dress, don't say you're a size 5. If you get the job and the wardrobe person tries to put you in a 5, you'll be sorry.

THE CASTING DIRECTOR

One of the five important items you need to write down when you get that call from your agent is the name of the casting director. After arriving at the audition, look for the person who seems to be in charge and, when the time seems appropriate, introduce yourself. If there is an assistant, also make sure you introduce yourself and be very pleasant. Most of today's casting directors were yesterday's assistants. Jot down any names you'll want to remember so you can review them later. You'll probably see those people again, and knowing their name can put you in a very good light.

The casting director or assistant may have some instructions for you to follow at this point. Be sure to be very attentive and listen carefully. If you don't understand something, ask.

Waiting rooms are usually adjacent to the actual audition room, so keep the noise down. If you see an old chum in the waiting room, keep your greetings at a low audio level. Don't use your time in the waiting room to socialize. Remember why you are there. Use this valuable time to study the script.

If the casting director seems to be a little on the harried side (an occupational hazard), don't get defensive or drop that smile. Try to get out of the habit of being caught up in other people's stress. Just smile, and be polite and charming. The casting director's problems with scheduling have no bearing on you, so don't let them affect you. Be sure not to add to any problems the casting director might have. Don't ask to use the telephone or ask directions to your next appointment or whatever. Try to be remembered as pleasant, unobtrusive, and totally cooperative.

THE SCRIPT

Now that you've signed in and introduced yourself to the casting director and/or assistant, you're ready to get a copy of the script and start to work on it. When you pick up your audition script, there may also be a story-board taped to the wall. A storyboard is a pictorial, scene-by-scene outline of the action in the script. It can give you an idea of what they have in mind for the action, the characters, the setting, the clothing, the attitude. Study the storyboard first before you start to work on the script. It will answer some questions that may come up. If you have any questions about either the script or the storyboard, make sure you ask.

There are five commercial categories, but before we deal with each of them in detail, here are some basic rules and tips that you can use in every audition.

Are there special words or abbreviations on the script that I should know?

A few. You'll usually find them on the left side of your script, but there may also be some in the copy. They're there to help you in your audition by telling you the size of the shot, whether the words are said voice-over by an announcer, whether you are outside or inside, and so on. If you know what they mean, you'll be able to use them to your advantage, so learn them now:

Video: what we see—usually camera directions

Audio: what we hear—usually the actor's words

VO: voice-over—an actor's voice, off-camera

OC: on-camera—what we see, the visual image

MOS: without sound—silent (stands for "mit out sound")

CU: close-up

TCU: tight close-up

ECU: extreme close-up

MCU: medium close-up

MS: medium shot

LS: long shot

WA: wide-angle shot

Two Shot: two people in the shot

Three Shot: you can figure this one out

Super: superimpose—when one image is placed on another, much like a double exposure. (At the end of a commercial, they will very often superimpose the product or logo on the screen with the final picture.)

Diss: dissolve—when one scene blends into the next

Cut: when one scene abruptly changes into the next

Int: interior

Ext: exterior

Alt: alternate—usually a reference to alternate dialogue or scene

Logo: slogan or product name

SFX: special effects

Hero: the product (not you)

Should I try to memorize the copy?

No! Unless you have a hundred-percent sure, no-effort, never-fail photographic mind, don't even try. The audition isn't a test to find out who can memorize the most words in the least amount of time. The actor who tries to remember all the right words finds himself concerned with only that and little else. If anything, try to remember the first and last lines (the attention-getter and the closing) so you can say them without looking down at the script.

Every time I audition with an actor or actress who says he or she has the copy memorized, I cringe with apprehension. Ninety-nine times out of a hundred they will not get the words right; nor will they get their cues right. If their cues aren't correct, it puts additional strain on me to try to salvage the continuity of the scene. One good thing is that they look so bad trying to recall their lines, they tend to do a poor acting job. And that means they won't get a callback and I just might.

THE AUDITION ROOM

What should I expect when I walk into the audition room?

Don't expect anything. The room may be filled with clients, agency people, production people, a director, a casting director, a videotape machine and operator—or it may have just one person in it. When you enter the room, smile at everyone, introduce yourself, shake hands, if they are offered, and hand over your composite and résumé to whoever seems to be in charge.

A casting director in Los Angeles once told me that when he first started, a well-known actor came to him for an audition. When the actor entered the audition room, there was only the casting director and his video camera. The actor, thinking the casting director was just someone hired to tape the audition, was very rude, remarking how awful it was that they didn't even have anyone important to watch the audition. The casting director didn't introduce himself and forgot to hit the record button during the audition. Be nice to everyone!

Again, keep a good attitude. If it seems as though the director or casting director is giving everyone a hard time, take advantage of it. If you have a great attitude, smile, and look like you're having fun, you may be the only actor seemingly not affected by all the negativity—and you may just get the job.

Be prepared for some small talk that always seems to happen at the outset. You can ask questions about the product ("Is this a new kind of Tinker Toy? I used to have a great set when I was a kid . . ."), the commercial ("I've seen your Tinker Toy ads on the air. They're very clever. Whoever thought to use that elephant standing on . . ."), or the ad agency ("I noticed from the copy that you're from the Iowa office. Aren't you headquartered in Des Moines? I lived there for three years when I went to the University . . ."). You don't even have to talk about the business. Something as mundane as "Isn't it a beautiful day? Y'know, I even saw a rainbow on my way here this morning . . ." is okay. Remember to keep your opening small talk short and on the positive side. You should be able to get a feeling of how far you should go. One line is usually enough unless they encourage more. Don't be a motor mouth.

First impressions are the strongest. You are auditioning for the commercial as soon as you enter the room. Project sincerity, confidence, warmth, interest, and success. Say only positive things. Be up. Be full of energy. First impressions are called "first impressions" because they only happen once.

If you have trouble in the small-talk area, don't despair. Many people do. Get together with other actor friends (or at least some sympathetic nonactor friends) to rehearse and practice a few opening lines. Go through some audition small talk and see how you do. Give each other constructive criticism. It's a lot easier to see what other people do wrong than to spot problem areas in yourself. Believe me, with a little rehearsal effort, you'll make small talk look effortless during the actual audition.

THE ACTUAL AUDITION

Once you're in position to begin the audition, the first thing you'll be asked to do is "slate."

What's the slate?

When you audition in front of a videotape camera, whether there are other people in the room or not, you'll be asked to verbally slate (to identify yourself on the tape) before you begin the actual audition.

So what should I do?

Wait until the videotape operator gives you the cue to start. The operator will either say "now," "speed," "action," or just wave in your direction (don't wave back). At that point, make sure you're wearing your best smile, look at the center of the lens, take a split second, and say your name clearly, as if you're proud of it. Remember that people can tell a lot about you by hearing you say your name. You can also get a little extra time on camera by saying something like, "Hi, my name is Arnold Anybody" or "I'm Arnold Anybody and I'm represented by Starmaker Limited." Some casting directors prefer that you *don't* mention your agent during your slate, so log that information down in your little book so you'll always remember it. Most actors make the mistake of using the slate to merely telegraph information. Don't lose this opportunity to demonstrate who you are and to give them a taste of your unique personality. Be proud of your name.

The camera operator will then either continue to let the camera run or stop the camera before the audition itself. Either way, make sure to take the time you need to collect your thoughts before starting the copy.

What do I do if I'm auditioning with another actor?

Don't let your partner's shyness, gregariousness, abilities, or lack of abilities affect you in any way. You are being auditioned on *your* merits, so don't look at yourself as a team member. No matter what your partner does, just be pleasant, keep that smile, and stay positive. Even if your partner and the casting director or director seem to be the greatest of friends, don't let it intimidate you.

Personally, I would rather audition with someone who does not have the best skills as a commercial actor. The human eye can only look one place at a time, and I'd prefer that the director, casting director, or client look at me rather than my partner.

Usually only one person out of a two-person audition will make it to the call-backs.

In a two-person audition, you will need to relate to your partner and be nice and friendly, but don't worry about him or her. Keep your concentration on the task at hand.

I've found that you can attract a lot of attention when slating with another actor by following a few simple rules. Any stage director will tell you that movement draws more focus and attention than speech. When you and your partner are both asked to slate, turn your head to your partner, smile, and magnanimously indicate that he or she may go first. Keep looking at your partner until he or she is finished, then turn your head back to camera (with that same winning smile) and do your slate. You'll not only look polite, generous, and friendly, but you'll have those all-important people watching *you* during most of the videotape replay later on. Try this one before you use it, though. It can backfire if you're not sure what to do.

AUDITIONING WITH CHILDREN

Children can be particularly difficult to work with for any number of reasons. Here are some tips that will make it easier:

- Depending on the size of the child, kneel down and put him or her in front of you, to one side of your face or the other. In most scenes, the child will be playing with something or eating something, so you both will be facing the camera. If the child gets behind you, all the camera will see is the back of your head.
- Take command of the situation during the audition. Don't be afraid to touch the child (tell the child you're going to) and physically put him or her where it works best for you.
- Children can sometimes take over the audition completely. Just be friendly but a little on the firm side. It will make them more secure and make you look more like a parent.
- If the child isn't doing what he or she's supposed to do, let the casting director do any correcting. Keep your composure, your winning smile, and recover any way you can in order to carry on with the continuity of the reading.
- Working with kids can be frustrating, but remember that it's frustrating for all your fellow actors. Just listen to the directions you are given and do your best.

"I was a fourteen-year-old boy for thirty years."
Mickey Rooney

Many actors will try to get to know the child a little before the actual audition. Some actors may even try a little horseplay. Be careful that you don't establish a too-cozy relationship—it may be counterproductive during the audition. I've always found it much easier during the audition if I assume the role of an uncle rather than the role of a buddy. If I know I'll be auditioning with a toddler, I'll bring a little wind-up toy or a gadget for him or her to play with. Don't give it to the child too soon. . . . Children that age have very short attention spans.

USING PROPS

What about using props during the audition?

Whenever logically possible, rehearse with and use real props. If you're auditioning for a coffee commercial, don't hand your husband an imaginary coffee cup. Look around the audition room. Nine times out of ten there'll be a cup. Use it! Acting is not pretending. Even Marcel Marceau can't make a client see a cup that isn't there. One casting director I know in Los Angeles refers to an imaginary product in an outstretched empty hand as "the claw."

Whenever you use a prop, make sure that you've rehearsed with it. Decide when and how you will use it, and then get rid of it, when you're through with it. Otherwise it becomes a hindrance rather than a prop.

It is always wise to carry a handbag or a briefcase to auditions. In it you should have a pair of glasses, a scarf, loose change, dollar bills, a checkbook, pictures, a wallet, a pencil, notepad . . . a multitude of items you can use for props. If the script calls for you to show your wife how much money you saved on the dog food, you can hold up real money. This helps you two ways:

- It gives you something concrete to do during the audition.
- It helps your credibility. When the client sees your audition or your audition tape, he'll think to himself, "Something's more real about that actor, I don't know what it is, but something's more real. Let's hire him."

Actually, my wife taught me the importance of using props. On her way to a Lipton Lite Lunch audition she bought a package of Lite Lunch and stuck it in her purse. When the audition copy called for the character to produce the product and solve her hunger problem, she pulled it right out. The casting director thought she was clever, the advertising

*agency and the client loved it, and Suzy got the job.
Moral of the story: If you go on a Coke audition, stop
and buy one! (Hide it, though. You don't want the
other actors to steal your idea.)*

USING CUE CARDS VERSUS USING THE SCRIPT

Usually there isn't a choice. In different geographic
areas they use one or the other. In Los Angeles, for instance, cue cards are always printed up for you, even
though you first see the copy on a script in the waiting
room.

The advantage to using cue cards is that your head
is up and your face automatically cheated toward the
lens. The cards are there to help you and make your audition better. If they don't seem to be written very
clearly, just remember that all the other actors have the
same disadvantage. Physically, the lines will be written
out and spaced differently from the script, so the copy
will look a little different. Be sure you rehearse aloud
once before they turn on that camera to record your
audition.

If you absolutely cannot use cue cards, then ask if it
would be okay to use your script. You'll almost always
do better, however, if you practice and use cue cards.

When rehearsing or reading hand-held copy, circle
your lines in pencil so that your eyes can easily find the
next set of words to say. It makes the usual two-char-
acter copy look only half as difficult. In spokesperson
copy, circle the opening and closing lines for easy, quick
reference. If there are cue cards, and the hand-held copy
is only to be used for rehearsing in the waiting room,
circle your lines or the opening and closing anyway. It
tends to break down the script and make the segue to
the cue cards easier.

When you're reading hand-held copy, fold the paper
so that only what you need to see shows. Folding the

101

script to the smallest possible size will not only keep your paper from shaking during your audition, but you'll be able to move the copy higher so your eyes won't have to look so low to find a line. Make sure you've read any stage directions on the left side of the page before folding the copy.

Whether you are using cue cards or hand-held script, it's most important that the camera and/or the people watching your audition get a clear view of your face. Always angle your face toward the camera (or them) so that *both* your eyes can be seen. If you're holding a script, try to hold it just high enough so that the camera sees your entire face, not the top of your head. Don't hold it off to one side, either. Practice at home in front of a mirror and see how you do.

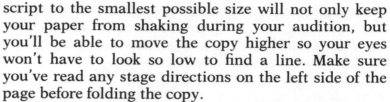

THE AUDITION CAMERA

Most television-commercial auditions are recorded on videotape so that casting directors, advertising people, clients, and directors can review them and make their choices at a later time. The audition camera is a casting-office fixture and something that we actors will always have to deal with. Learn to look at the camera as a friend that can help you get a call-back and not as an intimidating machine. Remember that everyone (including the camera) *wants* you to do well and they would love to stop their search for the "right person" with *you!*

The camera, even though it may be ten feet away from you, can zoom in to a very close shot of your face. Any movement from side to side or shifting of body weight can look very strange during playback. Plant your feet firmly and stand equally on both of them.

• Start your smile long before your slate, keep it up during your slate, and finish up your reading with it. Don't "turn on" when you think the camera is running. You may be fooled. Keep that smile and energy up from the time you enter the room until you're on the way home.

• If people in the room ask you questions while the camera is running, always talk to them as if they were inside the camera lens. If the tape is running and you keep looking one way or another to talk to different people, you'll look quite foolish during the playback. This takes some practice. It may feel awkward during the audition, but it will look terrific when they review the tape later.

If you have a video camera and recorder at home, have a friend help you tape some mock interviews and auditions. It will be an incredibly valuable experience and will start getting you accustomed to the camera.

103

MORE TIPS ABOUT THE AUDITION

There are still a lot of them!

• You should approach any audition enthusiastically. Be happy that you've gotten this far. For every actor who finally gets to audition, there are a lot of less-fortunates who were overlooked. You aren't there by chance. Your name was suggested somewhere by someone, and the casting director said yes.

• Speak clearly, a little louder than you normally would in conversation, and enunciate your words. Note where the microphone is and try not to bump it or make shuffling noises with your script or a prop that might distract from your audition.

• If you have a regional dialect of some sort, get rid of it! There are any number of speech and dialect teachers for you to work with—maybe even at your local college. It's nice to be able to do dialects when called for in specific auditions, but a heavy accent will limit the roles you can play.

• Even if you feel you aren't right for the part you're auditioning for, never let anyone know you feel that way. Just do your best during the audition. Many times an actor who isn't right adds a favorable twist to the character and the character is rewritten slightly to fit that actor. If you aren't right for this job but you do audition well, the casting director may call you back another day for a job for which you're perfect. Never try to cast yourself in or out of a role. Let casting directors do it. It's their job, not yours.

• Be sure to listen to whatever the person in charge has to say. Give that person your full, undivided attention and hear the instructions. Assume that if any additional instructions are given to you, they are extremely important. What seems to peeve casting directors most is having to repeat what they just explained. Listen!

• If you don't understand something in the copy or a verbal instruction, make sure that you ask *before the reading*. Don't take a chance—you'll appear uncertain. If you don't understand whether the commercial is supposed to be humorous, don't know the meaning of a word or a pronunciation, then ask. You may only get one chance, so you might as well do it right.

• Again, the audition may begin with (and sometimes entirely consist of) impromptu talk. This is very common in auditions, so be prepared for it. You may be asked the old stand-by question that seems to be a favorite with people in the industry: "Tell me a little about yourself." Look into the camera (if it's being taped), pick an area that may interest whomever you're talking to, be personal, and expand on it. Whatever you do, don't recite a list of credits. If you want to review this part of the audition, go back and reread pages 96 through 98. Be prepared.

• Even though you should never try to memorize all of your copy, some eye contact with your partner and the camera is extremely important (see Categorizing the Commercial, page 126). You should memorize as much as you comfortably can of the opening and the closing. Delivering that first line looking directly into the camera starts the reading with a bang; finishing up in the same way can mean a call-back and a job.

1. SLATE

LOOK AT CAMERA

2. OPENING LINE

DO NOT LOOK AT COPY
(MEMORIZE)

3 BULK OF COPY

REFER TO COPY

4. LAST LINE

DO NOT LOOK
AT COPY (MEMORIZE)

• Even though you've memorized your opening and closing to give them extra impact, make sure you don't die out on the rest of the copy. There's always a tendency to lose energy, particularly in spokesperson copy, about halfway through the script. Take your time and make each part count.

• If you must wear glasses to read the copy (particularly when reading spokesperson copy), make sure you slate with them off, do your memorized opening with them off, put them on for the bulk of the copy, and then take them off for your memorized finish. This will let them see you both ways and it will add a dimension of authority to your reading. As a general rule of thumb, however, it is good to wear contact lenses. Many actors even carry phoney glasses to use for the above effect or for a character look. If you try this technique, make sure you practice it. It sounds simple, but it takes a little dexterity and practice to make it look effective.

1. SLATE

2. OPENING LINES

3. BULK OF COPY

4. LAST LINE

• If you're auditioning with a partner, take a look at *your* next line toward the end of *their* line. It is more important to get your cues in on time and get the copy right than it is to have full eye contact. Make sure you know what your cues are. Also take a look at the other set of lines—you may be asked to switch parts.

• Don't be afraid to take your time before starting your reading. After your slate, look at the first line or phrase you've committed to memory, look up, and start. Be absolutely sure you're ready before taking the plunge.

• If you make a mistake during the reading and have a chance to tape again, make sure you verbally go over the place where you made the mistake. There's a reason the mistake happened, so be sure to fix it before proceeding.

• Be aware that adrenaline always makes everyone speed up, so force yourself to slow down. You'll probably only have one chance, so take your time and make sure it's right.

• If you immediately get off to the wrong start—stop; ninety-nine percent of the time you'll be able to try again. On the other hand, if you fluff a word, just keep going and forget about it. Don't dwell on your mistakes. No one ever cares about one mistake. They will care about the second, third, fourth, and fifth mistake you make because your mind is on the first one. Don't draw attention to it. Just forget it.

• If they ask you to do the reading more than once, be happy that you get another chance. It means that they're interested. Try to find a different way to do the reading. Don't carbon-copy what you did before. Show them how versatile you are.

• If *you* feel that you'd like to try something a little differently and ask to be taped again, make sure that you do something different! Most actors will ask to try something new and then repeat exactly what they just did.

ACTING TECHNIQUES

How about some acting tips on reading commercial copy?

A lot of well-trained actors, who've worked in television, in film, and/or on stage, find the world of television commercial acting both different and difficult. In each of these related but decisively different mediums, the audition as well as the performance varies greatly. Actors who work onstage, for instance, are accustomed to being very broad in their delivery. Actors who are used to playing to the last row in a large theatre might just bellow themselves out of the audition room. The key is to focus that energy into a two-inch camera lens and make it much more intimate. On the other hand, an actor who is used to acting on a much more subdued level, such as a soap opera, may have to bring *more* energy and broadness into the audition.

If you audition for a commercial the same way you audition for a role on stage, in a television show, or in a film, most likely you won't get the job. Many of the acting principles apply to all forms of acting, but there are also specific rules peculiar to each subcraft.

You mean all those acting classes I've been taking are worthless?

Of course not. The goal of any actor, whether he or she is doing Shakespeare, a soap opera, or a soap commercial, is to take someone else's words and make them sound like they're being said for the first time. Acting is the art of being real under the most unreal of circumstances. Lee Strasberg once said that an actor is a person who has the ability to be private in public. Any acting class that helps you to that end is invaluable.

How can you be "real" doing a soap-commercial audition?

Good question. Let's use an example of a typical audition and see how real we can make it look.

REAL ACTING VERSUS PRETENDING

The opening instructions on the script tell you it's an anniversary dinner with husband and wife in a restaurant. As the husband presents his wife with a gift, a waiter comes by and drops food on the wife's dress. We then cut to the wife successfully washing her dress in the detergent. It comes out clean and all is saved. There are no written words in the script, and you're expected to improvise the situation.

Your task is not to *pretend* anything. If you make believe that the two of you are a married couple in a restaurant having your anniversary dinner, you'll spend a lot of time trying to invent expository dialogue that will come out stilted and false. You'll also run out of things to say very soon.

Well, then, what do we say and do?

Rather than trying to *tell* us what's going on, *show* us that a relationship exists between the two of you. Say words that are the result of a real thought. Reality is the other actor; pretending is the character. Don't pretend. Really take a good look at the other actor in the scene and find something about him or her that you honestly like. Put a smile on your face and just tell him. Look at her and tell her that her hair is very pretty, and touch it. Look at him and tell him that you love the shirt he's wearing. Take his hand in yours. You aren't script writ-

ing or being informative. You're not pretending anything. You're just being real. All of a sudden the scene
takes on a new dimension called reality. And the people
watching the audition or the audition tape will see that.

Sounds easy!

It is! All of a sudden, you're not acting with an
imaginary character, you're merely dealing with another actor. You can stop pretending she's your wife and
you're having an anniversary. Then the scene becomes
remarkably easy to play. In the same vein, when you are
supposed to give your "wife" the anniversary gift, actually give the actress something. Take off your ring or
your watch and present it to her. It looks much more
convincing than handing her some air.

The best way to prepare for commercial improvisa-
tions is to take a class in improvisation. The teacher will
give you a scenario and you'll have to come up with the
action and the dialogue. You'll learn to think on your
feet, and if you try to deal with the reality of the situation as much as possible, you'll do very well.

*In an acting class I once took, we did a particu-
larly clever exercise that has always stuck with me.
The teacher asked three actors to improvise that
they'd all been arrested and were in a holding cell in*

111

jail. Before they'd even had a chance to ask a question, he shouted "Go!" and they were on their own. Everyone started to explain why he had been arrested. "I'm in for rape, murder, and extortion. What're you in for?" "Oh, I need a fix!" "I'm a notorious killer!" and so on. The teacher let the scene go on for about twenty minutes, and even though the scene initially got a few laughs, all three actors ran out of things to say after the first two minutes.

The teacher then announced that he was going to whisper the "secret of acting" into their ears. He took each actor aside and quietly told them to do some real things while they divided their time between sitting and walking. He told one to alphabetize all the makes of cars he could think of, silently, in his head. Another he told to count the holes in the acoustic ceiling, but not let anyone know what he was doing. He told the third one to recite chronologically to himself the names of every teacher he'd ever had. He then told the one actor to groan when he hit a certain number of acoustic holes, another to yell "Damn!" when he thought of a teacher he didn't like, and another to let out a chuckle when he'd counted ten cars, fifteen cars, and so on.

What happened was truly a miracle. We saw actors onstage who could have been inmates of a jail. They all could have won acting awards, and they weren't pretending to be in a jail at all. They were doing real things and therefore being real.

"That was my one big Hollywood hit [*Wizard of Oz*], but in a way it hurt my picture career. After that, I was typecast as a lion, and there just weren't many parts for lions." Bert Lahr

What's all this I hear about the actor "becoming" the character?

No one ever really becomes a character. If the actor playing Othello really believed he was The Moor, they'd have to get a new leading lady every night. You are you. You've been angry, sad, happy, afraid, gregarious, shy. If you do an audition where your character is depicted as a shy person, don't *pretend* to be shy. There've been times in your life when you were shy. Figure out what

physical characteristics accompanied that feeling. It's very difficult to pretend to be shy but very easy to lower your voice, speak hesitantly, avert your eyes when someone speaks to you, shuffle your feet, twiddle your thumbs, and generally make yourself as small as possible.

You can never become someone else. Why try? Someone once asked Spencer Tracy if he ever got tired of just playing Spencer Tracy. Mr. Tracy snapped back at him: "Just who would you like me to play? Humphrey Bogart?"

Once these basics become second nature, a whole world opens up. You'll be able to do things you never thought possible. It's an exciting craft!

Here are some more tips to keep in mind:

• If you're doing a commercial with another actor, listen to that actor and what he or she is saying. Listen with more than your ears. Listen with your eyes, your face, your whole body. You'll find that whatever you're

113

saying, your words will flow much easier because there's some logic to them. You're not only responding to *what* the other actor said but *how* he or she said it. Most acting is purely reacting. If you're really listening, you won't be acting only during your lines—you'll be in the scene the entire time.

• Practice saying thoughts rather than reading words. Read copy from magazine ads into a tape recorder and listen to yourself. If it sounds like you're reading words, then you've got work to do. Use inflections in your voice and try not to sound flat. Doing vocal exercises before an audition can help, but the only way to become more proficient at reading aloud is to practice reading aloud.

• If you're going to emphasize certain thoughts or words in the copy, don't hit the small connecting words like *but*, *and*, *so*, and *if*. Emphasize descriptive words. If you are performing in a food-related commercial, emphasize words like *yummy*, *delicious*, *crunch*, *juicy*, and *scrumptious*.

ATTITUDE CHANGES (OR TRANSITION POINTS)

Attitude changes are the key points in the commercial for the actor. Most commercials are divided into six basic parts, as follows, and attitude changes usually occur at the transition from one part to the next. Let's take a quick look at how a typical slice-of-life commercial is constructed:

ATTENTION GETTER

PROBLEM

SOLUTION

RATIONALE

RESOLUTION

CLOSING

115

These six different areas may be very easy to spot or very difficult to spot. Understanding the six parts of a commercial will help you break it down and make it easier to work with. In almost every piece of commercial copy (even spokesperson copy), there are what we call attitude changes, or transition points, for each character. These can be a change from negative to positive, dismayed to pleased, unconcerned to aware, whatever. Look for the exact point (or points) at which your character changes tack. Look for the obvious ones. Transition points are important and usually occur when the solution is presented and/or when the problem is resolved. Decide when and where your character's transitions are and what each transition is; then make the change abruptly and execute it fully. See if you can spot any transition points in this script:

SPOKESPERSON: You'd be surprised how many people would bet that it's easier to get a telephone number by dialing 411 than it is to use the phone book. Fact is, that's not a good bet. It's easier and faster to find and dial a number than it is to go through the operator. Next time, use your phone book. You'll save yourself time.

Now, where is the first major transition point? If you guessed just before the words "Fact is . . . ," you're right. Actually that attitude change would happen just after the period of the preceding sentence, but before you start to say "Fact." The words up to that point are the presentation of the problem. Then we begin with the solution to that problem. Try delivering the first part of the text, up to the transition point, as a matter-of-fact statement. After the statement is made, stop, smile, establish eye contact with the camera, and start the transitional sentence on your new tack.

When you become more skilled, you'll be able to find these changes or transitions where others won't. A very good commercial actor could easily find and make use of more than one attitude change in this copy. Finding those points is the easy part. Making full, abrupt changes is the hard part. Be careful to avoid "sliding" from one change to the next.

Here's an example of doubles dialogue. See if you can spot the transition points for each character:

DOUBLES COPY
Married couple on a Sunday morning at home.

SUZY: Y'know, there's this guy in my aerobics class . . .
JOHN: Yeah?
SUZY: . . . well . . . he's got dandruff!
JOHN: Why don't you just tell him?
SUZY: John, I have something to tell you.
JOHN: You mean . . . ?
SUZY: [Nods yes]

Scene dissolves to a shower scene with John using the product.

A few days later.

JOHN: Y'know that "guy" in your class?
SUZY: Yes?
JOHN: How's he looking these days?
SUZY: Absolutely wonderful!

Obviously, John's first attitude change (he's not too swift . . .) is just after Suzy's third line. John must make that transition clearly and distinctly *after* the last word of her speech. Suzy, on the other hand, has her first transition point after his second line. She needs to make that transition before her next words are said. There are certainly other attitude changes for each character, but these are the obvious initial ones. Again, when you get to the point of transition—stop, make your change fully, then proceed with your next line. The *action* comes first—then the words follow. Act, then talk. (You sneeze first, then you say "excuse me." Not the other way around.)

1. ACTION   2. SPEECH

PHYSICAL MOVEMENT

Whenever possible, use physical movement within the frame line of the audition camera. Think of it as talking with your hands. Any movement outside that frame line is not only wasted, but it becomes distracting. You might ask how wide the shot is so you'll know how tight you need to make your gestures.

The illustration on page 119 shows how Arlene's hands might be used effectively with our spokesperson copy. Also notice her transition point.

Because your hand gestures must be confined within the frame line, this exercise might seem a little awkward. Try it until it looks and feels natural. When you do use your hands, never put them between your face and the camera. If the gestures seem too much, let the casting director tell you they're too much. You'll get a chance to do it again.

Let's take another look at the doubles copy on the previous page and see what we can do in the physical-movement department.

DOUBLES COPY
Married couple on a Sunday morning at home.

SUZY: Y'know, there's this guy in my aerobics class . . .
JOHN: Yeah?
SUZY: . . . well . . . he's got dandruff!
JOHN: Why don't you just tell him?
SUZY: John, I have something to tell you.
JOHN: You mean . . . ?
SUZY: [Nods yes]

You'd be surprised how many people would . . .

. . . bet that it's easier to get a telephone number by dialing 411

. . . than it is to use the phone book . . .

Fact is, that's not a good bet.

It's easier and faster to find and dial a number than it is to go through the operator.

Next time, use your phone book.

You'll save yourself time.

119

Scene dissolves to a shower scene with John using the product.

A few days later.

JOHN: Y'know that "guy" in your class?
SUZY: Yes?
JOHN: How's he looking these days?
SUZY: Absolutely wonderful!

James Dean's first professional acting job was in a Coca-Cola commercial.

Since John appears to be responding to his wife absent-mindedly, he needs to find something that would be distracting him. A magazine or a folded newspaper is always a safe bet. Since we know that movement draws more attention than speech, it might be a good idea for him to turn the page just before his partner says her first line, then turn it again before speaking at all. This will draw attention to John and put him in the scene even before the lines start. A good time, incidentally, to drop the magazine or newspaper would be just before the line "You mean . . . ?"

John could also add movement by being physically turned away from Suzy at the onset of the spot and then turning back to her just before his realization line "You mean . . . ?" Suzy, on the other hand, might choose to begin her first "Y'know" turned slightly away from John, and then turn toward him for the finish of the line.

These are just a few of the many opportunities in this copy for physical movement. Keep in mind that most actors don't use physical movement to their advantage. Also keep in mind that most actors don't end up working.

One of the most effective actions an actor can take during an audition is to physically make contact with another actor. Because slice-of-life commercials deal with the relationships between characters (husband and wife arguing over deodorant, two neighbors talking about fertilizers, father and son discussing the merits of fluoride), the act of one actor touching the other can show us an immediate relationship even without words. How the physical contact is demonstrated will not only

establish a relationship, but it will tell us what the relationship is.

> *During the shooting of a Safeguard Soap commercial, one of the advertising people asked me if I knew why I'd been selected as the husband. I said that I had no idea. His answer was that I had touched the actor at the opening of the commercial audition. They all felt that I had immediately established a loving relationship with the other actor. All I did was touch her hair and shoulder just before my first line. It worked!*

The Suzy-John doubles copy contains plenty of opportunities for touching. Suzy could come up behind John and run her finger along his sleeve, then pull it away for her second line. John could come up behind Suzy for his first line after the shower scene and touch Suzy's shoulder or her hair. Suzy could embrace John or kiss him on the cheek after her last line of copy. If it is done well, anyone watching the tape playback should not be able to tell whether the two actors are old friends or had just met that day.

Utilizing touch in the spokesperson copy can also be quite effective. An inventive actor might bring along a small phone book to use as a prop in our first piece of copy (page 119). The actor could bring the phone book up into the frame just before saying, ". . . than it is to use the phone book." Then the actor could touch the telephone book with his free hand after the word "operator," and before the first word of the next sentence. Try it.

As with all physical actions, don't make the mistake of "suggesting" a touch. Decide what you are going to do, when you are going to do it, when you are going to stop doing it, and then do it fully.

VERBAL AND PHYSICAL OPENINGS AND CLOSINGS

Another device that is most effective during the audition is the use of both a verbal and a physical opening and closing.

Sir Laurence Olivier, one of the greatest actors of all time, in his first professional stage appearance tripped over the scenery and fell into the footlights.

Let's talk about the physical opening and closing first. Before you say the first word of copy, you should do something physical. For the doubles copy, it was suggested that John turn a page of his magazine or newspaper and Suzy physically turn toward John. The spokesperson can always use a turn into the camera before starting the copy. A physical closing for the spokesperson copy could be a finger tap on the phone book. It could also be a wink. A hug by the actors reading the doubles copy would be a perfect physical closing.

The verbal opening and closing can be used in conjunction with or separate from the physical. Before you say your first word, you can make a sound of some sort. A grunt, a whistle, clear your throat, coughing—these all help to establish what you're doing at the opening of the spot. Suzy, in the doubles copy, could say "ahem" before speaking, to show that she's uneasy approaching John about his cruddy hair. John, on the other hand, could be whistling a tune softly under his breath to show us that he's happy it's Sunday morning and he doesn't have to go to work. The spokesperson selling the phone book might let out a small sigh or a "huh" before starting. At the end of the doubles copy, John or Suzy might sigh with pleasure or say "ohhhhh." The spokesperson might consider a barely audible chuckle at the end of the copy.

Try eavesdropping on conversations in restaurants or at the market. You'll hear a lot of verbal sounds, or "colors," of conversation. People personalize their speech with grunts, gasps, giggles, and groans. Openings and closings are great places to use them, but they can work well in the rest of the copy, too. These special touches are what make the copy yours.

Never make your verbal openings or closings actual words. Copywriters tend to get defensive when you start writing copy into the script. Anything not in *Webster's* is fair game.

Practice these verbal and physical openings and closings until they look as if they were written into the script. Again, the important thing to remember is that very few actors are going to do them. But then again . . . very few actors work.

THE ASIDE

Another technique some actors successfully use when auditioning with spokesperson copy is called "the aside." It can give the effect that the spokesperson is telling the viewer a secret. To do an aside, simply lean into the camera or step slightly toward the camera before delivering the conclusion of the script. Some actors even take a quick look right and left to see if anyone is "listening" when they do it.

Now, let's go back to our spokesperson copy. The aside would be performed during the second-to-last line, just after the words "phone book," but before the

beginning of the last sentence. It's been working onstage for a very long time. Give it a try.

SPOKESPERSON: You'd be surprised how many people would bet that it's easier to get a telephone number by dialing 411 than it is to use the phone book. Fact is, that's not a good bet. It's easier and faster to find and dial a number than it is to go through the operator. Next time, use your phone book. [*Aside*] You'll save yourself time.

ACTING WITHOUT WORDS

What if I don't have any words to say in the commercial?

Good! In narrative/story commercials and in no-line vignette commercials, you won't have any words to say. Don't feel that these types of auditions allow you to let down your energy or relax your presentation. It usually means that you must physicalize the action more than you normally would. You'll need to dig a little deeper into your bag of tricks to do something to be remembered.

Just make sure that your presence is felt. Even if you're auditioning as the neighbor (no lines) observing two other neighbors arguing over lawn mowers, your part is just as crucial as the others. Most good acting is good *re*acting, and reacting doesn't depend on words.

The use of verbal sounds to color your performance is not only allowed in the audition, but essential. Even though you won't have words to say, you need to bring your character to life. Use those verbal openings, closings, and fillers as needed. If you are hired as a principal actor, it makes no difference whether you have words to say or not. The pay's the same.

GO ALL OUT!

The biggest mistake actors make when auditioning is not being fully committed to whatever it is they do or say. Don't censor your first impulse—it's usually right on the money. Don't be laid-back, reticent, or noncommittal. Whether your character is a shy, stupid husband or an overbearing next-door neighbor, commit yourself

and go for it. There is very little room in commercials for subtlety. The audience has to find out who you are and what you're all about in the opening seconds.

In all the workshops I've ever taught, rarely have I seen anyone go too far with a character. To my way of thinking, there is no such thing as overacting. I've seen a lot of bad acting, but rarely overacting. Usually, actors do about twenty-five percent of what the script requires. When you work with them, they get

about ten percent closer each time. Unfortunately, you have only one shot during the audition, so try to go for one hundred percent.

CATEGORIZING THE COMMERCIAL

The script at your audition will most likely fall into one of the five categories we've already touched on. That category will have a great deal to do with how you approach your audition. Take a look at the categories below, identify them, and then go sit in front of your television set for half an hour. You'll see an example of each one. The five types of commercials using on-camera talent are:

- the spokesperson commercial
- the slice-of-life commercial
- the one-line vignette commercial
- the no-line vignette commercial
- the narrative/story commercial

There is also a category called the real-people testimonial commercial: These commercials do not show actors, but "real" people who tell of their experiences using the product. Since there are no actors used, there are no auditions for testimonial commercials. People in these commercials may be selected on the strength of their response to a taste test or by an interviewer in a grocery store or shopping mall. The commercial can be shot with a hidden camera or an exposed camera, but most advertisers realize that these "real" people can become "real" tense when confronted with a camera.

THE SPOKESPERSON COMMERCIAL

A spokesperson is a representative for a product. The product may be an idea or it may be an actual product. The spokesperson always speaks directly into the lens of the camera and talks to the audience on a one-to-

one basis, trying to convince the consumer that the product is good, better, or the best available. He or she may play the part of a convinced consumer, a specialist, an informed party, or the president of the company, but whatever the role, a spokesperson always speaks with authority. The actor must be knowledgeable, convincing, sincere, and well-informed, yet appear warm and

friendly. Well-known personalities such as James Garner, Karl Malden, Cheryl Tiegs, and Orson Welles have appeared as spokespeople who endorse cameras, travelers' checks, makeup products, or wine. Corporate bosses have been used with varying amounts of success, but Chrysler hit pay dirt when they used their own Lee

Iacocca. The majority of television spokespeople, however, are actors and actresses selling somebody else's goods.

The Toyota commercial reproduced below is a typical example of spokesperson advertising. In this case, as with many spokesperson spots, there was no storyboard printed. DFS–Dorland, Worldwide (the advertising agency) and Toyota Motor Sales, Inc. (the client) were both gracious enough to allow me to reproduce this script for my book.

TELEVISION COPY

dfs — *DORLAND, WORLDWIDE*

CLIENT:	**TOYOTA MOTOR SALES, INC.**	LENGTH:	:30
PRODUCT:	**COROLLA**	SHOW & DATE:	
TRAFFIC NO.		TITLE:	**"MAP"**
DATE TYPED:	**5/29/79 CALVELLI/PP/ea**	CODE:	

video	audio
Tight shot of Announcer. Pull back to reveal him walking on large map of world with price per gal stickpins. Anncr. stops by Corolla. Tag line. Music/ singers up.	Non consumare benzina. Don't waste gas. It's a world problem . . . and here's an answer: The best-selling car in the world. The Toyota Corolla. Take the Toyota Corolla 2-Door Sedan. Its engine is designed to energize every drop of fuel efficiently. And it's also the lowest-priced Toyota. It's the answer to a whole world of problems. Hey, when you got it, you got it. <u>MUSIC</u>: TOYOTA

Actually, this is one of the commercials I did for Toyota. It is also my favorite. It's the piece of copy I first auditioned with back in 1979 and has led to my doing more than five hundred commercials for them. Needless to say, I love this piece of copy!

Let's review a few things you might consider doing during an audition using this Toyota spokesperson script.

• Find out if the camera operator is going to widen out his shot after the opening line and how tight the shot will be at the outset. You always want to stay within the frame line.

• Try to memorize your opening and closing. If all you can safely memorize of the opening is *"Non consumare benzina,"* then only do that much. If you can memorize more, then do it.

• If you're not fluent in other tongues, you may not know which language the first line is written in. It will make all the difference in the world how you deliver the words. Ask. Once you find out it is in Italian, you can say the line as you imagine an Italian would. Use your hands when you speak. Overenunciate the words.

• The attitude change would probably occur after the word "problem," so stop, smile, and give them the answer to the world problem.

• When you give them the answer to that world problem, you might also want to point and look off-camera toward where the car would be, before starting the next thought.

• You'll notice that the script says "world problem" at the opening and "world of problems" at the end. The same gesture for both those bits of copy might work for you.

• Don't let your energy down during the bulk of the commercial. All that copy is important, so don't speed through it.

• You might want to try "the aside" for the last line of copy. It was written for that treatment.

**"After my screen test, the director clapped his hands gleefully and yelled: 'She can't talk! She can't act! She's sensational!'"
Ava Gardner**

• You also might want to try a shrug or a tongue click before the first line. Maybe a wink or a positive nod after the closing.

How's that for a few things to try? See what else you can think of.

THE SLICE-OF-LIFE COMMERCIAL

On the next few pages is an audition script and a storyboard for a thirty-second slice-of-life commercial. In this type of commercial, it's as though the camera were eavesdropping for a few moments into some people's lives. It has a very short, single-purpose story with a very discernible plot. As in most stories, it has a beginning, a middle, and an end. There is a problem presented—"Isn't there a towel strong enough to scrub?"; a possible solution—"Try Brawny!"; and a resolution—"Brawny, you make camping easier!"

In this kind of commercial, everyone apparently lives happily ever after because the paper towel, deodorant, foot powder, aspirin, toothpaste, or sleeping aid completely solves their emotional and physical problems, and their lives are altered for the better. Marriages are saved, sanity is secured, embarrassment is avoided. There's always a happy ending.

Some slice-of-life commercials have a serious tone, but most are written with a light touch. Unlike spokesperson commercials, the actors relate to each other and *never look into the camera* unless the script specifically says to.

My thanks to the William Esty Company and the American Can Company for their permission to use the script and storyboard for this Brawny Paper Towel commercial. This spot is a favorite of mine because my wife and I were both hired.

TELEVISION COPY

WILLIAM ESTY COMPANY
INCORPORATED

ADVERTISING

EAST 42ND STREET • NEW YORK, N. Y 10017 • 697-1600

American Can Company
BRAWNY PAPER TOWELS
:30 TV
"Campers"
ACNT 5173

<u>AUDIO</u>

1. <u>SON</u>: Dad!!

   <u>DAD</u>: Wait, Bobby.

2. <u>DAD</u>: (To wife) Isn't there a towel strong

   enough to scrub?

   (SFX: LOUD CRUNCH)

3. <u>BRAWNY</u>: There is one.

4. Try Brawny.

5. (SFX: MUSIC STING)

6. <u>MOM</u>: Strong enough for this griddle?

7. <u>BRAWNY</u>: Sure. Brawny's got (SFX: SMACK)

   scrub strength!

8. Even strong enough for that mess.

9. Because Brawny takes tough absorbent fibers

   and . . .

10. bonds them together tightly . . .

11. (SFX: SCRUBBING) for scrub strength.

12. <u>DAD</u>: Brawny, you make camping easier.

13. <u>BRAWNY</u>: Brawny.

14. And designer Brawny. Both with scrub strength.

131

WILLIAM ESTY COMPANY INC.
ADVERTISING ·TELEVISION

client | American Can Company
product | BRAWNY PAPER TOWELS
title | "Campers"
job no. |
date | 2/28/79

video

audio

1. OPEN ON COOKING AREA OF CAMPSIDE. TENT AND CAMPER BUS IN BACKGROUND. SON WITH FISHING GEAR BECKONS FATHER. DAD IS STRUGGLING TO CLEAN DIRTY GRIDDLE.

1. SON: Dad!!

   DAD: Wait, Bobby.

2. HUSBAND TURNS TO WIFE. BOBBY SEES BRAWNY. HIS MOUTH FLIES OPEN. HE POINTS UPWARD.

2. DAD: (to wife) Isn't there a towel strong enough to scrub?

   SFX: LOUD CRUNCH

3. BRAWNY ENTERS. SURPRISED MOM AND DAD LOOK UP.

3. BRAWNY: There is one.

4. MOM AND DAD STILL LOOKING IN AMAZEMENT AS BRAWNY BENDS DOWN.

4. Try Brawny.

5. BRAWNY PRESENTS TOWEL TO CAMERA.

5. SFX: MUSIC STING

video		audio

6. MOM AND DAD STILL LOOKING UP AT BRAWNY. DAD HOLDS UP DIRTY GRIDDLE.

6. MOM:

Strong enough for

this griddle?

7. BRAWNY SMACKS FIST.

7. BRAWNY: Sure. Brawny's got

(SFX: SMACK)

scrub strength!

8. CUT TO MAN'S HAND SCRUBBING GRIDDLE WITH BRAWNY. TOP PART OF 409 CLEANER IS VISIBLE.

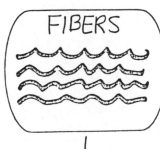

8. Even strong

enough for that

mess.

9. CUT TO FIBER DEMO.

9. Because Brawny

takes tough

absorbent fibers

and . . .

10. ACTION CONTINUES.

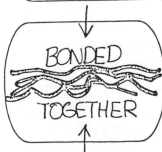

10. bonds them

together tightly . . .

SFX: SCRUBBING

video   audio

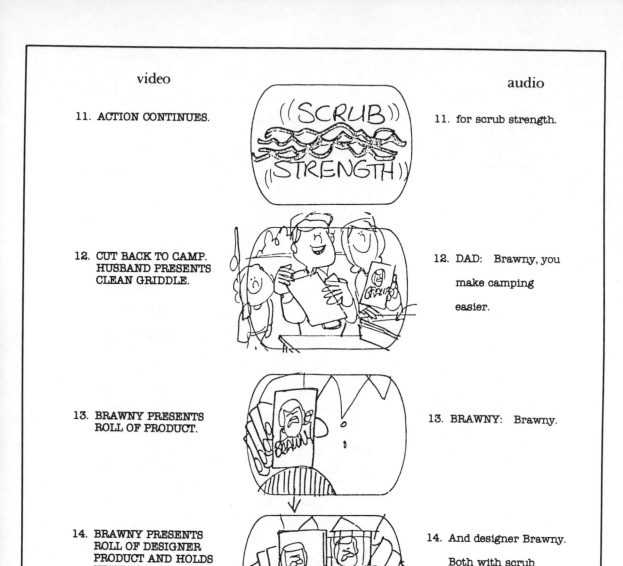

11. ACTION CONTINUES.   11. for scrub strength.

12. CUT BACK TO CAMP. HUSBAND PRESENTS CLEAN GRIDDLE.   12. DAD: Brawny, you make camping easier.

13. BRAWNY PRESENTS ROLL OF PRODUCT.   13. BRAWNY: Brawny.

14. BRAWNY PRESENTS ROLL OF DESIGNER PRODUCT AND HOLDS NEXT TO FIRST ROLL.   14. And designer Brawny. Both with scrub strength.

Now let's take a look at a few things that enterprising actors might be able to do with this copy during their audition.

• Because there's no indication of what the actors should be doing in the script, it's very important to take a look at the storyboard before the audition. If not, you

may not know that Dad is supposed to be cleaning the dirty griddle with a towel that's falling apart. And you wouldn't know that the loud crunch is supposed to be the Brawny Giant stepping in to solve their problem. Storyboards are very important.

• When the son "sees" the giant, he needs to make sure that he picks out a place way over the camera lens, either camera right or camera left, to look and point. This pointing makes us understand that he sees something and also gives the other actors a point of reference.

• Dad needs to be busy scrubbing something *with* something. Rather than pretend to be scrubbing, it would be best to use a handkerchief (or a paper towel you've gotten out of the men's room before the audition) and scrub your hand at the bottom of the frame line. Scrubbing your hand isn't as good as scrubbing a griddle, but it's a lot better than scrubbing air.

• Mom doesn't have any words until well into the copy, and it would be best if she weren't just standing there waiting for her first line. She could turn away from the other actors so that she would have some turning action to do when her husband asks her his first question. Or the actress could be packing some things into her bag. What she does isn't half as important as the fact that she is doing something.

• The obvious attitude change for Dad occurs after his frustrated line about strong towels, just after he physically looks to where the son is pointing. Mom's initial transition could be shortly before or after that.

• There's a great opportunity for the son to come out with a sound like "whew!" or "wow!" just before he says his first line. Dad could let out an exasperated sigh or grunt before his first line or after his "Wait, Bobby." Being careful not to actually say any words, Mom could begin to answer Dad's question to her before Brawny answers for her.

• All these actors must be sure that while they are astounded by the giant, they do not exhibit fear. This is very important because the giant represents the product and the product is always a positive thing to behold.

• After Dad says his last line, he could chuckle, the son could wave at the giant, Mom could hug Dad. (Or Mom could wave at the giant . . .)

See what else you can come up with.

THE ONE-LINE
VIGNETTE COMMERCIAL

The vignette commercial is a commercial composed of quick scenes using different actors. Each actor says a word or phrase (usually into camera) with energy and enthusiasm. It could be the name of the product or a word or phrase describing the product.

What follows is a typical one-line vignette commercial. The product, Alpine Yogurt, is fictitious.

Television Copy *video*	:30 Television	Alpine Yogurt *audio*
1. Open on snowy exterior scene of mountain cabin. Slow zoom to door.		1. (vo) All over the world . . .
2. Cut to woodsman eating Alpine.		2. . . . there's something that this man . . .
3. Cut to beach scene on Riviera. Attractive, thirtyish woman eating Alpine.		3. . . . this woman . . .

video		*audio*
4. Cut to tulip field in Holland. Eight-year-old girl sitting amongst flowers eating Alpine.		4. . . . this girl . . .
5. Cut to ballet-school scene in France. Confident eight-year-old girl eating Alpine.		5. . . . and *this* girl all have in common.
6. Cut to ECU of woodsman.		6. WOODSMAN: Alpine!
7. Cut to beach woman.		7. BEACH WOMAN: Alpine!

video		*audio*
8. Cut to girl.		8. GIRL: Alpine!
9. Cut to girl.		9. GIRL: Alpine!
10. Cut to product shot.		10. (VO) Alpine! (echo of *many* voices in unison.)

GREAT! FINALLY AN EASY ONE!

Looks like a pretty easy commercial to audition for, right? All you have to do is look at the camera, eat some yogurt, and say one word.

Wrong! Keep in mind that if it seems like an easy audition to you, it will also probably seem like an easy audition for everyone else. You can be sure that the competition for the job is just as stiff as for any other.

The instructions from the casting director or assistant will probably be something like, "You're enjoying your yogurt at the beach (in the field of flowers, wherever), and then you say 'Alpine!'" (Even though the commercial has you in two scenes, in the audition these will most likely be done as one scene.) Use any script suggestions and casting director's instructions, and then dig deep to come up with ideas that will make your audition stand out.

• They will probably expect you to pantomime eating the yogurt, so stop at the store on your way to the audition and pick up the product, and you won't have to pretend you're eating. (You can even claim it as a tax deduction—"audition prop.") You cannot imagine how much of an impact this makes on the people who have the ability to hire you. The surprising thing is that very, very few actors think to do this. (Take the food into the audition room in a paper bag. Don't let any of the other actors know what you're doing.)

• Dress properly for the part. Your agent has already told you who your character is and has given you a hint of appropriate clothing. If you're in doubt about the suitability of a particular garment, ask him or her.

If you're auditioning for the woodsman, wear your jeans and a flannel shirt. A long-john-type undershirt with long sleeves and suspenders might be welcome additions. Also see if you can find a knit hat to bring along. (Another item to hide from your competition.)

If you're auditioning for the woman at the beach, wear a bathing suit (conservative unless specifically requested otherwise) under some casual clothes. You can remove your street clothes in the audition room. Bring sunglasses to wear on your head (never cover your eyes) and a ribbon for your hair.

The two girls should do the same thing as far as clothes and props are concerned. A leotard and tutu for the ballet student or a Dutch-boy hat for the girl in the field are all plus points for clothing. If you can think of something unique, use it.

• Anything you can do to change your body position, expression, and attitude is useful. Opportunities for changes in this spot are easy to find, but make sure you do them, do them abruptly, and do them fully. Here are some obvious changes:

Start by *not* looking at the camera during the first part of the scene. Look at the yogurt, take a spoonful, *then* turn to camera for your line.

Change your look from a look of anticipation to a look of delight after taking the bite.

Change body positions from a slight slouch to an erect posture after taking the bite.

• Be aware that there's very little time to build a story here. You can't spend time putting on suntan oil, building a fire, picking flowers, or dancing. The copy says that your scene starts with your character eating yogurt and finishes with the word "Alpine!" Make the most of the short scenario you have. The focus here is not on the environment but on the character eating Alpine Yogurt. Start by eyeing the yogurt container in your hand; open it, look at and smell the contents, dip the spoon in, stir the contents, take the spoon out and look at the yogurt, put it in your mouth, taste it, and then *react* with the line. Also make sure you have something to do after the word "Alpine." Enthusiastically eating more yogurt would be the obvious choice.

• When you're doing food commercials, take tiny bites. Otherwise the lens of the audition camera might get a little cloudy when you hit the *p* of "Al*p*ine!" (Incidentally, *never* show in any way that you don't like the food or product.)

• As in other types of commercials, utilize sounds in reacting to the product. "Mmmmmmmm" is a great

Spencer Tracy began his theatrical career playing a robot.

one. Just don't say anything that sounds like a word. If it's in the dictionary—don't use it.

• When you say the line of copy, notice if there's an exclamation point after a word. Practice saying the word so that it comes out a positive statement and not a question. Always smile when saying the name of the product.

• The tendency for most actors is to hurry to the punch line. Everybody's going to be saying that punch line, so it stands to reason that it's what you do *before* the line that will get you a call-back.

THE NO-LINE
VIGNETTE COMMERCIAL

This is the same as the one-line vignette commercial, except there are no lines for the actors to say. The characters are usually caught "unaware" by the camera and then react positively to the product. These shots are often called reaction shots for obvious reasons. This type of commercial is used for soft-drink ads that show quick, high-energy shots of young people enjoying the beverage.

The storyboard for the Alpine Yogurt commercial on page 137–139 is a good example of the no-line vignette, if the last line is omitted and only the actors' reactions are shown. Go back and try the yogurt commercial without the line. You'll notice that by not having a line at the end of the spot, you are forced to rely on the full and complete transition you must make from *before* tasting to *after* tasting. Without the line, the change is even more apparent and important. All the other tips for the one-line vignette apply to these spots. (Even though there are no lines in this type of commercial, you should still use your "sounds.")

THE NARRATIVE/
STORY COMMERCIAL

While the vignette commercial features quickness, energy, and variety, the narrative, or story, commercial involves a simple story line. These spots are usually the most creative with regard to direction, writing, cinematography, and editing. They can be used quite effectively to appeal to the emotions of viewers and can sometimes be genuine tearjerkers.

The following is a pretty good example of a typical narrative/story commercial. Tenco is a fictitious brand name.

Television Copy	:30 Television	Tenco CB Radios
video		*audio*
1. Opening wide-angle shot of car on desolate highway at dusk. No other cars in sight. Headlights flick on.		1. *(haunting music up, mixed with solo car noise)*
2. Dissolve to wide-angle shot of same car. Very dark and ominous.		2. (SFX: *thunder and rain)*
3. Dissolve to same shot. It's raining heavily.		3. (vo) Some people think that a CB radio is just for truckers . . . or maybe just a toy . . .

4. Cut to driver of car. Woman, twenty-five to thirtyish, concerned look on face.

4.

5. Cut to gas gauge of car. Reading is empty.

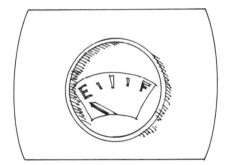

5.

6. Cut to driver. Obviously worried.

6.

7. Cut to car slowing down. Turn-indicators on to pull over. Car comes to a stop alongside road. Rain is heavy.

7. (SFX: *car sputtering*)

8. Different angle. Car alone on side of road. Emergency flashers go on. Another car speeds by.

8.

9. Cut to very worried driver. She tries starting the engine. No luck. She gives up in desperation.

9. (vo) . . . but at Tenco, we think a CB radio is the second most important thing you can have in your car.

10. Pull back from CU of driver to wide-angle shot. No cars in sight. Fade out slowly.

10. (vo) The first . . . is you.

Auditioning for this kind of commercial is a lot different from auditioning for any of the others. A commercial such as this one is really like a short movie, and the acting is on a much more subtle level.

The casting director or assistant will give you instructions like, "You're in a car, alone; it's raining and you run out of gas. You don't know what to do."

Let's see what you could do with this one:

• Dress accordingly. It's a stormy, rainy day, so wearing a scarf and a coat with a collar would make for some good props.

• The opening scene might be a good time to check

on the time. A wristwatch is a great prop for a lot of commercial auditions. Make sure you actually see what time it is . . . don't pretend.

- The script says that the character is first seen as the rain starts. Take a moment *before* you realize it's raining so that you can make a transition from happy-go-lucky to concerned. To make the transition even more effective, hum a tune or softly whistle to yourself before you react to the rain.

- You could go from a more casual sitting position to an upright one as the rain starts.

- The script indicates that there's a point where the character realizes she's almost out of gas. This will mean another transition from concern over the rain to seeing the gas gauge and becoming downright worried.

- Another transition is at the point when the car speeds by after you are stopped. Physically use your hand (within the confines of the car) to wave to it as it goes by. When you realize that the driver's not going to stop, make the transition from worried to frightened.

These aren't the only things you could do if you were auditioning for this spot, but they're a few ideas to think about. The more ideas you have, the more you can eliminate the less attractive ones. The more you can break down the action into moments and events, the clearer it is to the camera and the easier it is for you.

Now you have the knowledge to separate yourself from the majority of actors. Apply what you know and practice. It's up to you.

Acting is one of the most competitive professions in the world. There are a lot of actors out there looking for work. Talent certainly enters into the picture, but frankly, I've never been able to define what that word means. I don't know if talent can be taught; I tend to think it can't. Skills, however, can be taught. If there are seventy-five actors auditioning for a commercial and they all have the same amount of talent, it is the actor with the best skills who will get the job. So the question is—What can you do during the audition that the others won't do? The answer is to incorporate these tips and practice them over and over until they become second nature.

I learned these tips as a result of years of auditioning and watching other actors audition. The tips work. Take my word for it. They're used by a select group of actors who have something in common. They all work!

Practice at home. Get some commercial copy from magazines, TV, or from auditions, and work with it. Borrow or buy a videotape camera and recorder and try each of these tips on your own. Some are easy, some are not, but with practice none is impossible to perform. Just be aware that knowing about them and being able to recognize where they should be applied in the script is a lot different from actually being able to incorporate them during an audition. Practice.

AFTER THE AUDITION

Congratulations on successfully getting through that first audition! You just had your hardest. You'll soon find that each succeeding one will become easier and easier. Learn something new every time you audition, and remember it. Use that little book and write down everything worth remembering, and you'll be miles ahead of your competition.

Here are a few tips for after the audition.

• When you finish with the audition, no matter how you think you performed, just smile, say "thank you," sign out at the correct time, and leave. Don't comment on how you feel the audition went—not to the casting director, the actor you worked with, or others who are waiting to audition. If you want to shout for joy or cry your eyes out, wait until you get at least a mile away. Even if you are feeling negative, *look* positive.

• If you happen to be performing in a play in town, mention it to the casting director before you leave. Tell him where it is, and if he would like to see it you would

be glad to send tickets. Don't ask as though you'd be hurt if he didn't come. It lets him know you're working as an actor and gives him something to talk about when he's reviewing the playbacks with the clients.

• Never assume anything about your audition. The job you thought you were absolutely perfect for, you won't get a call-back on; and the interview you were certain you bombed may end up getting you the job.

• Don't make the mistake of calling everyone you know to tell them that you went on an audition. If you do, they will call twice a day to see if you got the job. Keep a low profile until you're certain that you're working. *Then* you can shout it to the world.

"I think I was good
when I was good."
Gwen Verdon

• Always have somewhere to go and something to do right after your audition. Don't go home and sit in front of the telephone. Visit a friend, jog, play racquetball or tennis, go shopping . . . anything, as long as you don't dwell on your audition. It's fine to figure out what you might have done better, but make the criticism as constructive as you can.

• As soon as you leave the audition forget it. Just go about your life and put it out of your mind. Figure out what it is that you can improve upon next time, and practice it.

All the years I spent auditioning and also teaching high school were beneficial to me in a lot of ways. The obvious benefit was that I could pay my rent because I had a steady job, but just as important was the fact that I really had to hustle to audition at lunchtime and then hustle back. I never had the time to dwell on the audition and how well (or poorly) I thought I did.

Actors all have funny (and not-so-funny) stories about getting jobs or not getting jobs. Here are a couple of my favorites:

After an audition for a Contac commercial, I thought I had failed miserably and asked myself why I was in the business. There had been some difficult action with a sleeping eye mask and I couldn't read the words while I was fiddling with it. Usually I just try to forget the audition, but this one was so bad

I thought if word leaked out there was a chance I would be washed up in commercials. In the middle of telling my wife about my miserable audition, my agent called to say I got the job. I guess everybody else had a hard time with the mask too!

Another time I was up for a lead in a television series at Universal Studios. After a number of auditions and call-backs, I was told I was "perfect," "exactly" what they were looking for, and that I had the job. I left the office with a smile on my face and a script in my hand and immediately called everyone I knew to tell them that I would be working on the series and would be very busy. A week later I had to call everyone back and tell them that I would have a lot of free time on my hands. Somebody else was doing the part! It's best not to say anything to anyone until you get your first paycheck. The best part of the story is that the show was a bomb.

THE CALL-BACK

What's a call-back?

A call-back is another audition for the finalists. If you do get a call-back for a commercial, it means that you're right for the job and could get it! Now they want to find the person (or combination of people) they feel would be best for this particular spot. If you've made it this far, relax. Now it's a subjective choice that has a lot to do with them and little to do with you.

How should I prepare for the call-back?

Again, relax! Whatever you did in the audition got you the call-back. Don't go out and buy a new outfit, get a new hairdo, or a face-lift. Wear the same clothes you wore during the first audition and wear your hair the same way.

What should I expect during the call-back?

Usually during the call-back there will be a few more people in the audition room. The clients and director may ask you to do it this way or that way. Just smile, listen to what's being asked of you, and do your best. Most likely you will be doing the same thing you did on your initial audition, but be flexible. You may be asked to read with different actors.

How soon will I know if I got the job?

Hard to say. It's possible to find out right at the audition—or you could wait a month. Many times they have to send the videotape cross-country to someone who will make the final decision. But don't worry about it. Forget the call-back. If you do get that call from your agent, it'll be a pleasant surprise.

THE JOB

Are there some more words or phrases we should be familiar with at this point?

Yep. Here you go.

Agency: The advertising agency employed by the client to develop an advertising campaign. They wrote the commercial you're about to do.

Client: The company that owns the product or service for sale.

Production Company: The company that was hired to shoot the commercial.

Director: The person in charge of the shoot. This person may also operate the camera. The director usually works for (or owns) the production company. Most television-commercial directors don't have a stage background but are likely to have experience in art direction or camera work. Many have a great visual sense and are wonderful at creating staging ideas but know next-to-nothing about acting. That is why you were hired.

A.D.: Not a reference to the date. This stands for the assistant director, who is in charge of many things and is your on-and-off-the-set liaison with the director. An A.D. signs you in and out, tells you when to go to lunch, notifies you when you need to get makeup and wardrobe, assigns your call time, and answers just about any question you might have. The A.D. can be a great help on the set. Learn his or her name and be friendly.

Producer: This term can mean a lot of different things. There can be a client producer, an agency producer, and a production-company producer all working on one commercial. Because they are all concerned with different areas of emphasis, they sometimes have disagreements. You should stay out of conflicts until they are resolved and then do what the director tells you to do. The producers will direct their thoughts and comments to the director, who will pass them on to you. (If you see them whispering in the corner, don't become paranoid; you've been hired because you were the best choice.)

Principal: All roles in the commercial in which the performer can be recognized or identified. Usually the audition is held for the principal roles, whether they are speaking parts or not. Extras are usually cast without an audition. They are the background people.

Talent: This term has no correlation with whether or not you have any. It merely means any actor who happens to be employed as a principal.

Availability: An inquiry as to your schedule on a particular day. A casting director will call your agent to see if you happen to be available for a commercial, but it is in no way binding.

Booking: An offer of employment for a specific job on a specific day. If you verbally accept (or your agent verbally accepts a booking), it is a binding agreement.

Conflict: A commercial you have done that is on hold or currently running and is of a similar product nature to another. An actor may not appear on-camera as a principal performer for conflicting products.

Downgrade: To hire an actor as a principal and move him or her to a lower category. If the commercial is edited so that you cannot be recognized or identified, you may be downgraded. This will eliminate any possible residuals (see The Money).

Upgrade: To move from the ranks of an extra in a commercial to that of a principal. This can happen if you are to play a recognizable or identifiable role or are given a line in the commercial that was not originally scripted. Advertisers avoid this like the plague. It means paying residuals to someone they didn't plan on.

Exclusivity: If you have a Toyota commercial on hold or currently running, you are exclusive to Toyota and may not do a Nissan commercial until released by Toyota (see **Conflict**).

First Refusal: A request to hold an actor for a given day. It is not binding for either the producer or you. It is more of a sign of interest than an availability request, and it is not as good as a booking.

Hold: An offer of employment. If you are actually put on hold for a day's shooting and end up not being hired for any reason, you are entitled to a session fee.

Holding Fee: The money that is paid to the actor every thirteen weeks for as long as the commercial is being held by the ad agency. This is usually the same as the original session fee.

"Procter & Gamble's television budget for 1985 was $800 million. In the average television-commercial budget, talent costs account for less than two percent of the total."

Session Fee: The money you are paid for the initial day's work on a commercial. It is usually a scale amount (see The Money).

Residuals: The monies paid to you for rerunning your commercial (see The Money).

Test Commercial: A commercial that will be aired in a small area and monitored for its effectiveness. You must be told that the commercial will be a test commercial before the audition.

Wild Spot: A commercial that runs on a non-network station, or a spot that runs on a network station but airs between scheduled programming.

Class A Spot: This is what we all hope for. It means that the commercial will run during prime time on one of the networks. Residuals are highest for this type of spot.

Weather Day: You are sometimes given a weather day if the location is outdoors. This means that if the weather is not right for the shoot and it does not take place, it will be postponed until the weather day. When this happens, you'll receive a half day's pay for each canceled day.

Location: Any exterior setting away from a studio set. If you go on location away from home, you'll be lodged and flown first-class, paid for by the client, ad agency, or production company.

Per Diem: Expense money given to you while on location for each day you are away from home.

Upstage: Away from the camera.

Downstage: Closer to the camera.

Camera Right: Your left as you look at the camera.

Camera Left: You can figure this out.

Blocking: Movement and action planned by the director.

Hitting Your Marks: The ability to physically stop on a preset mark or put down the product in an exact spot.

Cheat to Camera: To turn your face to the lens of the camera a bit, so that more of your face can be seen.

Key Light: A light specifically set up to highlight you. Make sure you're in this light and don't move out of it.

Wrap: The last shot of the day is over. Go home.

156

What's the day going to be like?

Included here is documentation of the schedule of events for a thirty-second Brawny Paper Towel commercial that both my wife and I appeared in. The script and storyboard are on pages 132–134.

TUES. MARCH 27:

10:00am - Agent calls Audition for both Squire and Suzy at Coast Productions (LA) for Brawny Paper Towels. Time—4:45 that day. Camping scene, husband and wife.

4:30pm - Arrive at Coast. Look over script.

5:10pm - Audition. Videotaped. (Thought we did poorly.)

8:00pm - Agent calls. Call-back for both of us the following day at 3:40.

WED. MARCH 28:

3:30pm - Arrive at Coast wearing same wardrobe. Look over script.

4:00pm - Call-back audition with director, clients. Videotaped again. (Thought we did a little better.)

WED. APRIL 11:

10:00am - Agent calls. Both of us got the job. Notified of wardrobe call and work date. (Unusual notification in two ways. First, it's very unusual for a real husband and wife to be cast as a commercial husband and wife; second, it was two weeks before we found out that we were cast.)

9:00pm - Suzy and Squire celebrate!

MON. APRIL 16:

11:00am - Wardrobe call at Coast. Brought all possible wardrobe for camping. Selections made. Map to location given out. Call time announced.

WED. APRIL 18:

8:00am - Arrive at location (approx. 1 ½ hour drive). Reported to Production Manager/Assistant Director.

8:15am - Reported to make-up.

8:30am - Got into wardrobe in the motor home.

8:45am - Reported to the director on the set.

9:30am - Rough blocking of movements and rehearsing of lines.

10:30am - Stood in place for final lighting and set adjustments.

11:30am - Touch up make-up and final rehearsal.

11:45am - Begin actual shooting of first set-up.

1:00pm - Lunch.

1:35pm - Back to make-up. Squire shaves again.
1:45pm - Back to the set. Continue.

5:35pm - Finish shooting last shot. (Called a "wrap" in the business.)

5:45pm - All actors record "wild lines." (Additional recording of audio "just in case.")

5:55pm - The A.D. calls a "wrap."

6:00pm - After "thank yous," two tired people head home.

Though you might be tempted to call this a "typical" workday, the longer that you're in the business, the more you realize that there *is* no day of work that could be called typical. Workdays are demanding and difficult. The more you are prepared for the difficulties and demands, the better you'll fare. When you finally do get a job, read and reread this section. It'll come in handy.

THE WARDROBE CALL

What do I need to know about the wardrobe call?

After you've been notified by your agent that you're definitely working, the person in charge of wardrobe will call you. This person (usually a woman) will tell you what clothing she's looking for and ask you what you own that might be suitable. Then you'll decide together what things you should bring in. She'll also take down your size and probably go shopping for some alternatives to show the client, agency people, and/or the director.

Here are some tips:

• Be as helpful as you can. Don't go out and purchase clothing, but do bring in anything you think they might use.

• If you bring in your own clothing, make sure it fits you. It isn't too helpful to have to tell them that the shirt they like doesn't fit you anymore.

• When you've finished talking with the wardrobe person, immediately get together all the clothes the two of you have decided might be appropriate. If you wait until just before the wardrobe call, you might not remember exactly what you decided to bring.

• Sometimes there is only one person at the wardrobe call, but most likely the client, agency people, director, and wardrobe person will all be present. This may be the first time you meet these people, so remember their names. Being able to greet them by name during the actual shoot can have lasting benefits. Also remember that all of them will probably be more familiar with you than you are with them. They've been looking at your audition tape over and over.

• You may feel a little like a mannequin during the wardrobe call (you basically are . . .). Don't let it bother you.

• Don't be offended that no one likes your personal clothes. Don't be offended if the clothes they select are terrible. Their taste, or lack of it, may be quite different from yours.

• There may be some disagreement among the powers-that-be about the suitability of a particular garment or two. Stay out of the discussion. You may think your input is important, but it's not. Interfering could unknowingly make an enemy.

• You'll be paid a fee (see The Money), for clothes you wear in the commercial that are your own property. Clothes that they buy are theirs. Don't walk off with them after the shoot is over. If you really like an outfit or a shirt, talk to the wardrobe person about purchasing it. The going rate (if they'll sell) is about half what they paid for it. If she doesn't want to sell it, don't pester her (the client may also wear a 40-regular . . .).

Sir Ralph Richardson was once told after an audition for Falstaff: "That is quite awful. It is senseless, badly spoken. You could never, never be any good as Falstaff."

MEMORIZATION

Don't make the mistake of not memorizing your part. When you show up on the set, know the script from start to finish—forward, backward, and sideways. Onstage, in television, and in film you can usually get away with being *almost* perfect. In a commercial, each word has been carefully chosen. There are sometimes more words to say than there is time to say them, so your mouth has to move a lot faster than your brain.

Memorizing commercial copy is much more difficult than memorizing an acting scene from a play. The words come faster, you're under the gun to get them all in on time, and there is no real rehearsal time before the shoot to link the words to the action. This is the toughest kind of memorization there is for an actor.

An actor has a certain confidence when he or she knows that the lines are memorized letter-perfect. You'll be better prepared to handle detailed blocking and complicated moves and end-of-the-day fatigue.

If there are any last-minute script changes (and many times there are), you'll be able to handle them if you're confident that you know your words. If you harbor the slightest doubt that the copy isn't etched in stone in your mind, those changes are going to throw you.

Anthony Hopkins couldn't remember his lines during his first outing as an actor and was fired.

Unfortunately, I'm a very slow study. It takes me a long time to memorize my lines so that they're perfect. I never want to make a line flub during a shoot. It is a frustrating problem, but at least I'm aware of it.

My solution is to start memorizing my words the second I get my hands on the copy. I type the script out on a small 4×6 piece of paper, highlight my lines, and go over and over them. If the commercial has doubles or multiple copy, I'll use a tape recorder to learn my cues. I particularly like to work on lines and cues while driving the Los Angeles freeway system. It helps pass the time.

If you don't really know how well you will do under pressure with your memorization, overdo it in the beginning. I've seen actors who brag about having a photographic memory and end up with a blank look in their eyes after a twelve-hour day.

THE MORNING OF THE SHOOTING DAY

You'll probably be nervous on the day of the shoot. It's just some adrenaline running around your system that normally isn't there. Savor it. All actors feel it before a performance. It's a feeling to be treasured. Use the energy to give a great performance. You were selected to do this job because you were the best.

Here are a few tips to make that morning go a little easier:

• Even actors who are seasoned performers have trouble sleeping the night before a shooting day. Don't make it worse by staying out late the night before or by eating four pizzas at a late dinner. Set yourself up for the best night's sleep possible.

• Set two alarms for your wake up. Make sure one is a windup, in case of a power failure.

• When you wake up in the morning, you may experience a sudden feeling of panic. It may also happen on the set, and it is a pretty common thing. It's almost like someone's going to discover that you don't have any talent and shouldn't be on the set. Remind yourself that you auditioned for this job and got it. Take a deep breath and tell yourself that you are the best choice.

• Leave yourself plenty of time to get to the shoot so you don't get frazzled because of a traffic snarl. There are no excuses for being late.

• Make sure you have everything you need for the day. You'll need whatever wardrobe you've been asked to bring, a hairbrush or comb, your script on a 4 × 6 card (see Memorization, page 160), and the directions to the shoot. Women should also take makeup (it might be possible to supplement the makeup artist's work), hair curlers, and hair spray. If your hair needs something special done to it, do it before you leave the house. Men should always take an electric razor along. You may not get a three o'clock shadow, but you might get a 6:00 P.M. shadow . . . or a 9:00 P.M. shadow . . . or . . . . It's very important that at the end of the shooting day you look just like you did at the start.

• Eat a good breakfast before leaving for work. If you don't, you'll be inclined to stuff yourself with food once you arrive. There's usually a table set up with all kinds of evil food designed specifically to sabotage you and your energy. If you have to eat something, stick to fresh fruit. Water, sparkling water, and fruit juices are a far cry better than coffee and soft drinks. The same holds true for snacks during the day. The wrong foods can affect or ruin a performance. Stay away from all these energy-roller-coaster-evils.

• You also might want to bring your own supply of water with lemon and honey mixed into it. This can help you out during a long day when your voice starts to give out.

What do I do when I get there?

- If you have a car and parking is limited, ask where you might put it for the day. Parking must be provided for you, so don't put your car in an illegal area and have it towed away or on the street at a one-hour coin meter. The assistant director can give you this information. He or she is also the person you report to upon arrival. Don't just assume the assistant director knows you're there. Find this person.

- The A.D. will tell you when to report to makeup and wardrobe. If the A.D. doesn't, then ask.

- You'll notice a lot of commotion on the set—a lot of people working hard and a lot of people hardly working. It doesn't mean that some are eager people and some are lazy people. Due to the nature of this business, certain groups of people will be working while others are not. Lighting people may be setting lights while sound people are inactive. Just stay out of the way of those who seem to be working, and watch. Keep those eyes and ears open and you'll learn a lot.

WHAT TO DO WHEN THE LOCATION IS OUT OF TOWN

Great! You get to travel for free. The flight and the hotel accommodations will be first class, so you should have a comfortable time. Make sure you have your ticket or know where and when to pick it up at the airport; know exactly where you will be staying and how to get from the airport to the hotel. Have a contact's name and number (both during the day *and* the evening) in case of a problem. If it's possible to hand-carry your luggage rather than check it through baggage, you'll save yourself time on both ends and reduce the chance of it being checked through to Iran. Save your receipts. You'll be given a per-diem amount for your expenses, or they'll reimburse you for your receipts. Either way, the IRS will want to know where the money went. Save those receipts!

If you frequently fly to different jobs, I strongly recommend subscribing to the OAG Pocket Flight Guide. It lists all the commercial flights in the United States and the times of departure. I've often had to change flights at the last minute, and this guide comes in quite handy. An updated guide is published and mailed to you once a month. The cost is forty-four dollars per year and is tax deductible. Write to: Official Airline Guides, 2000 Clearwater Drive, Oak Brook, Ill. 60521. Ask for the North American edition.

WORKING ON THE SET

What can I do to "fit in" on the set?

This is a tough one. Remember that many of the crew members have worked together before and they may be friends off the set. Just be aware that everyone new to this kind of situation will be feeling what you feel. (Remember that first day of school?) Be nice to everybody. Do what you can to get to know people. They probably won't make the necessary overtures, so it's up

to you. When they're not busy, talk to the sound people about what they do, when and how they got started, the equipment they have, and so forth. One thing's for certain—they do sound because they're *into* sound! Ask their advice on some equipment you're thinking about buying. Talk to the makeup artist. Ask about interesting jobs he or she has done.

Try to learn all you can about what each person does. If you do, you'll be remembered as a person who is interested and interesting. You'll make some valuable acquaintances and you'll be spending your idle time constructively. Who knows, on the next job you do, one or two of the same people may be on the crew.

The best way to have people enjoy you on the set is to do what's expected of you and do it well. Know your words, work hard, be accessible, friendly, and respectful.

Who's really in charge on the set?

Good question. The director is really the one in charge. Anyone who wants to give you direction must first go through the director. The purpose of this unspoken rule is to avoid situations where the actor will get conflicting information on how to do something or how to say something. If you find that you are getting information from more than one source, just smile and try to do what's asked of you. They'll eventually work out their problems. Any questions you have about staging or delivery should be aimed at the director.

You'll sometimes see a conflict on the set between the client, ad agency people, and/or the director. Stay out of it and don't let it affect you or your performance. These things happen all the time. You may also see a huddle of important people looking your way, pointing at you, and speaking under their breath in a concerned, sinister way. Don't worry. This has nothing to do with their choice of actors. It usually means that they haven't decided where to go for lunch and are talking over the possibilities. If they are talking about you, it's just to give the director their ideas about how the scene should be played, how a word should be emphasized, or how the product label needs to be turned correctly to camera. Don't get paranoid. You got the job.

For every director in this business, there is a different personality. Some directors like to work with actors, some do not. Keep in mind that his or her personality and style of working were developed long before you walked on the set. Just smile, do your best work, and don't let someone else's problems affect you.

*I've worked with a lot of directors over the years.
I've seen directors use their position to try to sleep
with actresses (and succeed); I've seen directors use
the foulest language imaginable with small children;
and I've seen them scream at an actor until he or she
could no longer perform. Some of the kindest people
I've ever known also happen to be directors. Just
be prepared. Directors are not required to take a
standardized psychological test. Some are nice. Some
are not.*

Will I get time to rehearse while I'm on the set?

Definitely. You'll probably be doing each scene many times to work out problems with lighting, timing, camera focus, product placement, and a hundred other things. This is not rehearsal time for you to work on your lines but a rehearsal to work out all the unknowns of the shooting day. While everyone else is working on their own areas of responsibility, make sure you are working on yours. You need to integrate your business and action with your already-memorized words, so that there is a relationship between the two. If you do your rehearsal work well, when everyone else is ready to go you will be too.

Once you've worked out what you're going to do, the director will want a number of variations. It's not uncommon to do a line or a piece of business a hundred times. If the director asks you to change the timing of something you're doing or the delivery of a line, make sure you try it on your own before trying it on-camera.

When you rehearse or are asked to "run through the copy for time," there may be a tendency not to do it full out. Resist that temptation. Do full movements; give full-out readings. If you don't, the rehearsal will do you no good.

One of the most difficult things for an actor to do is repeat what he or she just did a hundred times and not vary the reading, business, or timing. It takes careful

**"God makes the star. God gives them the talent. It is up to the producers to recognize that talent and develop it."
Samuel Goldwyn**

167

work during the rehearsal period to iron out and lock in what you're doing. Use the rehearsal time and use it well. Concentrate!

What does "hitting your marks" mean?

During the rehearsal process, there will be someone literally putting tape on the floor or on set pieces for camera focus. If the actors and the product aren't in place, right on the button, the camera focus will be soft and the shot won't be any good. To make things even more difficult, after the rehearsal process is over and the shooting is about to begin, the tape marks are *removed* so they won't be in the shot. That's why your rehearsal process is so important.

A good trick is to try to keep your own visual marks in mind, using existing set pieces, smudges on the floor, or whatever. This takes a little practice but isn't too hard. Concentrate.

Hitting your marks is a particularly difficult thing to do as a beginning actor and seems to grow easier with experience. It's a way to either drive a director crazy or make him or her want to work with you again.

Very often, when you're watching a television show or a soap opera, you'll see an actor look down at the ground in thought as he moves across the set. He's not in thought . . . he's looking for his marks!

What about stunts in the commercial?

If there are dangerous stunts to do, there should be a stunt double to do them. Don't be a hero. Every year actors are maimed or even killed because they were doing something unsafe while working. This gets to be a little sticky at times. You want to work, but at the same time you're concerned for your safety. Use your best judgment, and if something appears to be too dangerous, it's best to say no. Better to lose a day's work than lose an appendage. Normally, if there is to be an

unusual feat, the actor will be asked beforehand during the audition process whether he or she can do it. Make sure you know what you're in for if you agree to do the job. Once on the set, it's a little late to say no. Make sure you personally check safety rigging and have clear in your mind exactly what's to happen in stunt-type situations. Just because the camera operator has no qualms about hanging from a rope dangling from a helicopter, it doesn't mean you don't. Never think "macho" on the set. "Macho" is another word for "dumb."

What about working with children?

Children can make a shooting day difficult. There are limitations imposed on everyone because of on-the-set schooling and the strict guidelines set up by the governing authorities of each state. But, most of all, they are just kids and usually act just like kids.

Leave any directing of the children up to the director. Let nothing shake your positive attitude and you'll do fine.

What about working with animals?

This is the same as working with kids, only they don't have to go to school. Don't get too friendly with the animal, and listen carefully to the animal trainer, who will be on the set. Above all, be careful.

Is there any secret to shaving off tenths of seconds when reading copy?

When Glenn Ford was once asked by a commercial director to deliver his lines at a faster rate, he replied: "Son, I've only got two speeds. The other one's slower."

If you are doing spokesperson copy and need to shave a tenth of a second off your reading, just give the reading with the same delivery you have been using. When you get to the last phrase or sentence, hurry it up just a touch. No one will notice any difference in your reading, and they'll all think you're a brilliant actor. If you need to shave two-tenths, do the same thing with the last *two* phrases. The trick is to make sure the rest of the copy is always consistent. Concentrate on consistency during rehearsal time.

Anything I should do just before they roll camera?

Set yourself up for the first piece of business you're going to do and focus in on the line. Do it just like you did during rehearsal. You'll do fine.

The assistant director will usually ask for quiet (or sometimes yell for quiet), then tell the sound person to roll sound (who will respond with "speed"), and tell the camera person to roll camera (who will respond with "camera's rolling"). At this point the slate will be put in front of the camera and usually clicked to make sure sound and video are synchronized later on. The director may then ask for quiet again or just say "action."

At that point, you should wait a split second so your dialogue won't overlap with the director's "action," then start.

Two things may happen to unnerve you a bit. When the sound person is given the instruction to roll sound, he or she will also push a button that either blows a horn or sounds a loud buzzer. Either can be disconcerting. Also, it gets deathly quiet at this point. The slate can be a bit unnerving too. If the camera is focused on your face for the opening, they may put the slate right in front of your face and then bang it together. It's not to scare you, so just put up with it.

It's a good idea to start a bit of relevant body movement just before the director says "action." It warms you up a bit for the scene, and you won't be coming from a dead stop as the scene starts.

OVERTIME

This is good. It means you're making more money. Commercial shoots can sometimes last a very long time. It is not a good idea to make plans for that evening. If you have an important engagement after the shoot, you will end up worrying about being able to make it all day long.

I was once playing Hero in A Funny Thing Happened on the Way to the Forum *onstage at South Coast Repertory in Southern California. I auditioned for (and got) a Right Guard commercial that was to shoot in San Francisco, the same day as one of the performances. I double-checked with the production company to see if I would be able to make curtain time, and they assured me that there was no problem.*

I worried all day long and didn't do my best work. We finished late, I made it to the airport, but the plane was grounded in San Francisco with mechanical trouble and I was forced to run to another terminal for a flight to the Los Angeles airport. I called the theatre and told them to have a car waiting at the curb (they weren't real pleased) and took off. By the time the plane landed, I was a nervous wreck. They picked me up in Los Angeles and then proceeded during the late rush-hour traffic to make the forty-mile trek to Orange County on the freeway shoulder at ninety miles per hour (while I changed into my costume). I made my entrance during the overture and gave one of the worst performances of my life. Two bad performances four hundred miles apart in one day!

WRAP TIME

Wrap time can be a time to relax after a busy day. It can be a good time to socialize and reinforce those names you learned during the day. There is often hard liquor, beer, and/or wine on the set after a shooting day. It's fine to have a beer or a glass of wine, but be sure to draw the line at one to leave behind a very professional image. If you need a second drink, have it at home. Word travels very fast in this business. Be sure to still be as polite and nice as you were during the day.

Congratulations! You got through your first workday and you're now a professional actor. Those you worked with were impressed at your preparation, your dedication, your professionalism, your sincerity, and your friendliness; let's hope it leads to other jobs.

THE FOLLOW-UP

How soon after I do the commercial will I see myself on TV?

Maybe never. Many commercials run nationally, many run regionally, many run locally, many run in a test market, and many don't run at all. Your agent will know the intended future of the commercial, but the best thing is to forget about it! As soon as the job is finished, start to work on getting the next one.

I once did a test commercial (a commercial to be televised in a particular geographic area and monitored for its success) for Coast Soap. Following my own advice, I promptly forgot about it until one night, two years later, I saw it on the air.

Another time I filmed a spot for Breck Shampoo on a Friday, and it was airing nationwide the following Monday!

What about thank-you notes?

A great idea! It never hurts to be courteous. Write short notes to the casting director, the director, the client, and the advertising people. Make sure the note is short, to the point, and not cute.

Is it possible to get a copy of the commercial?

It usually is, especially if you do write a thank-you note. Just wait until the commercial gets on the air and drop a short note to the advertising people. Sometimes you'll have to pay a small fee for the 16 mm. print, but usually it'll be free.

I began doing this when I first started doing commercials. I wrote for a copy of every commercial I did, whether it got on the air or not, and ended up with a couple of one-hour reels when they were all spliced together.

Should I keep a file on each commercial?

Another great idea! You're learning fast. Just keep that little notebook around and keep track of the job, the casting director, the production house, the director, the clients, the advertising people, names of crew members, and so forth. With luck, you'll be seeing these people again somewhere, sometime. Everybody likes to be remembered.

THE MONEY

Wine maketh merry: But money
answereth all things.

Ecclesiastes

How pleasant it is to have money.
Arthur Hugh Clough

Money is indeed the most important
thing in the world.
The Irrational Knot

Put money in thy purse.
William Shakespeare

A fool and his money is soon parted.
James Howell

Everybody likes a little money; some people like a
lot of it. The purpose of this final chapter is to let you
know how (and how much) commercial actors are
paid—and, most important, to advise you that there are
ways of keeping many of those dollars.

How, and how much, do I get paid?

Roughly, it goes like this: As of the 1985 commercials agreement,* an on-camera SAG–AFTRA actor earns a basic $333.25 per eight-hour day. Overtime is, of course, extra; over eight and up to ten hours is time and a half; over ten hours is double time. Meal periods are deducted from total hours. That initial $333.25 is what is called a session fee.

Every thirteen weeks, the producer of the commercial must pay you an additional fee equal to the session fee. This is called a holding fee and is paid to maintain your exclusivity to that particular commercial and category. Remember that you cannot perform in more than one commercial in the same category—takeout foods, cosmetics, automobiles, whatever—during your exclusivity period. If the producer fails to send you that holding fee within the prescribed amount of time, you are automatically released and may open up that category. If a mistake is made it can be a very sticky and costly situation, so don't assume anything until your agent places a call to see if you are, in fact, released.

If and when the commercial does get on the air, it can do so in any number of forms, which mean varying amounts of payments sent to you, called residuals. The actual breakdown is much too complicated to go into here, but your residuals basically depend on the estimated number of viewers watching during the time the commercial is aired on that channel. The different categories have names like wild spot, class A program commercial, regional commercial, local commercial, dealer spot, test-market spot, and so on. Generally speaking, the best type of commercial to be in is one that will run nationally as many times a day and as many days as possible.

It's not uncommon to do a commercial for a "buyout." This is an arrangement among the producer, actor, and agent agreeing upon a set number of dollars to be paid each thirteen-week cycle instead of residuals. Ask your agent about this one.

*SAG–AFTRA will be negotiating their new contract in 1987.

177

You are also paid for any wardrobe fitting at $41.66 per hour. The penalty payment to the actor who is held over one hour on a commercial audition amounts to $20.83 per half hour. If you wear your own clothing in a commercial, the fee paid you is $12.50 per outfit.

All monies due you are usually forwarded to your agent, who takes out his ten percent from the gross amount. (The only exceptin to this is an AFTRA job done for the minimum scale. The ten percent to the agent on a session fee can be over and above your $333.25.) The agent then mails you a check for the remainder. Agents are entitled to ten percent of all session fees, holding fees, and residuals. They are not entitled to any of your wardrobe-fitting money, commercial-audition overtime money, or wardrobe-use money.

Who keeps track of how many times my commercial is on the air?

Believe it or not, the people who hired you.

How do I know I'm not getting cheated?

You don't, but most of the mistakes happen only on the local level. Somebody's looking for a quick filler at Channel 3 and your spot is thrown on.

The advertising agencies have an agreement with their clients. They tell them that for a certain amount of money they will put a particular commercial or campaign of commercials on the air in a number of markets. They show them (in great detail) when, where, and how many times the spot(s) will air. You then are paid according to that report. The clients won't cheat you because they're not in a position to, and the ad agencies won't cheat you because if your commercial plays *more* than they've indicated, they pay for that air time and don't get any return from the client. Unless it's a mistake, a local station won't play it, because nobody's paying to have it played.

I once did a commercial for an amusement park near Los Angeles. I was notified that the commercial was off the air, but about a month later, one of my students (I was teaching at the time) said that he'd seen the spot the night before. I quizzed him about the time and channel and then called the union. They checked the station's log and discovered that they had indeed run that spot. I was paid a handsome sum for a penalty and holding fee. (I bought the student a cheeseburger.)

"Actors pay in advance." A sign in a turn-of-the-century pub window

179

How much money does the usual commercial make in residuals?

There's no such thing as the "usual" commercial. You can make a session fee and that's all—or the commercial can play a lot, and you can make a lot. My advice is to do the job and forget it. If it plays, you get a surprise. If it doesn't, you don't get disappointed.

The least amount I've ever gotten on a commercial was a session fee of $136.00 (back in the old days). The most money for an individual spot was $22,259.51 for Shake 'n Bake, $22,607.53 for Coast Soap, and an even $31,000.00 for Coca-Cola. These top grossers were each on the air for close to four years. I figured out that the average figures for me were somewhere around $2,400.00 per spot. Again, the best thing to do is do the commercial, take your $333.25, and forget it!

How can I keep the money I make?

Actors are notoriously poor money handlers. Many of them hire business managers (who take about fifteen percent of the gross dollars) to put them on a budget and pay their bills. With a little intelligence, you can not only save that fifteen percent, but also gain a little pride in the fact that you do handle your own money, and you can handle it well.

It seems as though actors are in either a feast or famine situation. This is the nature of our business, so you have to be intelligent with your money. Here are a few tips to follow:

• Don't quit your job when you decide to become a commercial actor. Even if you have a lot of luck, it takes time to build up a few commercials to the point where you can make a living. Also, if you resign from a job, it is questionable whether you are entitled to unemployment benefits.

• If you do make some money, don't run out and spend it on all those things you've always wanted. And don't buy anything on time, thinking that the residuals will cover the payments. They never do.

• The important thing to do (particularly in the beginning) is to save money! If you have another job, then put all your acting money in a savings account. A credit union (both SAG and AFTRA have credit unions) is a great place to put money. They pay higher interest than banks and it's a little farther away than your local bank, so you have to think twice about withdrawing funds. No matter how little or how much you make, always put ten percent of your gross paycheck into savings. You'll be surprised at how fast that money grows.

I started doing this when I first began acting. No matter where the money came from (teaching, acting, mowing lawns, whatever), I'd put ten percent (or more) into the credit union. Within a few years' time, I had enough for a down payment on a house, then a small triplex, then an apartment building, then another. Because of that initial ten-percent commitment, I've been able to make enough investments to guarantee the future of my family.

• One of the most important things for a commercial actor (aspiring or otherwise) to do is to keep com-

"Don't ever forget what happened to the man who suddenly got everything he always wanted. He lived happily ever after." Willie Wonka

plete and accurate records of monies spent to further his or her career. All these items are tax deductible if you have records. An IRS audit is never pleasant, but it can be most unpleasant if you don't have records.

• Be aware that your agent, in most cases, has your power of attorney. That means you've given him or her permission to cash your checks. Whenever you receive money, keep track of who it's from, what it's for, when you got it, and how much it is. Make a list of each commercial and keep very accurate records. When your earnings statements come in the mail at the end of the year, it's very easy to match up how much you made with how much they said you made.

My first commercial agent "misplaced" over five hundred dollars in residual money from an Olympia Beer commercial I did. It took me about ten telephone calls to find out where my money was. But I found out, and I got it back (with interest). He left the business shortly after that. I always wondered how many other clients who didn't keep records had their money misplaced.

Congratulations! You are now filled with the know-how very few people have to make acting in television commercials both fun *and* profitable. *The rest is up to you. Good luck! I'll be looking for you on television.*

APPENDIXES

A Quick Course in Commercials, from Concept to Completion

Listing of Agents and Union Offices

APPENDIX A
A Quick Course in Commercials, from Concept to Completion

Now, whether you're in the process of finding an agent, looking for that first job, or trying to stay working, it will help you to take a brief look at how a commercial is made from the initial concept . . .

. . . to the finished, on-the-air commercial.

The client (Schmaltz Beer) decides at some point that he wants to advertise his product on television to boost sales. He employs an advertising agency (Shtick Ad Agency, Inc.) for the job. Account executives at Shtick and marketing executives at Schmaltz then decide who they want to buy their beer (age group, socioeconomic status, sex, and so forth) and how they can best approach that particular group.

After this decision is made, Shtick Advertising has a copywriter come up with specific commercials. The copywriter's presentation will usually be in the form of a storyboard—a large sheet of cardboard with a series of drawings depicting the different scenes in the commercial.

After possible revisions, when Schmaltz is pleased with Shtick's storyboard, he gives the go-ahead for production.

At this point, several production companies are contacted for competitive bids. These are the folks who will actually film the commercial.

After the production company is selected, the "creative teams" from Schmaltz and Shtick begin to work with the production company, finalizing all details such as location, casting, and so forth.

In New York, most of the large ad agencies have their own casting departments. In most other places around the country, separate agencies are employed to do casting. In either case, the casting directors call agents asking for specific types. Lists are submitted to them by the agents, and then they choose who they will audition. Casting people are very important people. Even if you are not yet represented by an agent, you can and should mail (or, if possible, drop off) your photo and résumé to casting agencies for consideration. This is much more an accepted thing to do in New York than it is on the West Coast, but it's a good idea regardless of where you happen to be pursuing your career. The worst thing you can do is get a "no thanks." Even when you've got an agent, don't hesitate to drum up a little business yourself.

Finally, a cast is selected through a series of auditions and call-backs. At this point, the commercial is ready to be produced—and the cast, the creative team, and the production people assemble on the shooting day. During the day of filming (usually a long one) the creative teams of both Shtick and Schmaltz and the production people all give their various (and varying) opinions of how to put the finishing touches on the spot.

Many of the same people may stand over the shoulder of the film editor some time later, each selecting his or her favorite take from the thousands of feet of film actually shot on the shooting day. Then music, sound effects, voice-over announcer, and special effects are added.

Finally, the commercial is finished. The result is truly advertising by committee.

APPENDIX B
Listing of
Agents and
Union Offices

Thanks to the SAG Board, Hollywood, for permission to use their list of agents. This list is constantly updated, so contact your local chapter every few months for the most current one.

AGENTS FRANCHISED BY THE SCREEN ACTORS GUILD

LOS ANGELES

A Special Talent Agency, 6253 Hollywood Blvd., Los Angeles, CA 90628; (213) 467-7068

Abrams-Rubaloff & Lawrence, 8075 West 3rd, Los Angeles, CA 90648; (213) 935-1700

Actors Artists Agency, 435 South La Cienega, #201, Los Angeles, CA 90648; (213) 205-0720

Agency for Performing Arts, 9000 Sunset Blvd., #315, Los Angeles, CA 90669; (213) 273-0744

Aimee Entertainment, 13743 Victory Blvd., Van Nuys, CA 91401; (818) 994-9354

All Talent Agency, 2437 Washington Blvd., Pasadena, CA 91104; (818) 797-2422

Altoni, Esq. Inc., Buddy, 3355 Via Lido, #355, Newport Beach, CA 92660; (714) 851-1711 or (213) 467-4939

Alvarado, Carlos, 8820 Sunset Blvd., Los Angeles, CA 90669; (213) 652-0272

Amsel & Assoc. Inc., Fred, 291 South La Cienega Blvd., #307, Beverly Hills, CA 90211; (213) 855-1200

Applegate & Associates, 1633 Vista del Mar, #201, Los Angeles, CA 90028; (213) 461-2726

Artists & Junior Artists, 4914 Lankershim Blvd., North Hollywood, CA 91601; (818) 763-9000

Artists Group, Ltd., 1930 Century Park West, #303, Los Angeles, CA 90667; (213) 552-1100

Associated Talent International, 9744 Wilshire Blvd., #306, Beverly Hills, CA 90212; (213) 271-4662

Athletes Registry, 2221 South Barry, Los Angeles, CA 90664; (213) 477-8202

Auer, Miles Bohm, 8344 Melrose Ave., #29, Los Angeles, CA 90669; (213) 469-2751

Ball, Bobby Talent Agency, 8484 Wilshire Blvd., #235, Beverly Hills, CA 90211; (213) 852-1357

Berzon, Marian, 336 East 17th, Costa Mesa, CA 92627; (714) 631-5936 or (213) 207-5256

Blanchard, Nina, 1717 North Highland Ave., Los Angeles, CA 90628; (213) 462-7341

Bloom, J. Michael, 9200 Sunset Blvd., #1210, Los Angeles, CA 90669; (213) 275-6800

Bresler & Associates, 15760 Ventura Blvd., #1730, Encino, CA 91436; (818) 905-1155

Bridges Talent Agency, Jim, 1607 North El Centro, #22, Los Angeles, CA 90628; (213) 874-3274

Button, Iris, 1450 Belfast Dr., Los Angeles, CA 90669; (213) 652-0954

Carey-Phelps-Colvin, 121 North Robertson, #B, Los Angeles, CA 90211; (213) 659-6671

Carroll Agency, William, 1900 Olive Ave., Burbank, CA 91506; (818) 848-9948

Cassell & Levy, Inc., 843 North Sycamore Ave., Los Angeles, CA 90638; (213) 461-3971

Cavaleri & Associates, 6605 Hollywood Blvd., #220, Los Angeles, CA 90628; (213) 461-2940

Chutuk & Associates, Jack, 9908 Santa Monica Blvd., Beverly Hills, CA 90212; (213) 552-1773

Cinema Talent Agency, 7906 Santa Monica Blvd., #209, Los Angeles, CA 90638; (213) 656-1937

CNA, 8721 Sunset Blvd., #102, Los Angeles, CA 90669; (213) 657-2063

Commercials Unlimited, Inc., Sonjia W. Brandon's, 7461 Beverly Blvd., Los Angeles, CA 90636; (213) 937-2220

Contemporary-Korman, 132 Lasky Dr., Beverly Hills, CA 90212; (213) 278-8250

Coralle, Jr., 4789 Vineland Ave., #100, North Hollywood, CA 91602; (818) 766-9501

Cosmopolitan Talent & Model Agency, 8142 West 3rd St., Los Angeles, CA 90648; (213) 655-9952

Creative Artists Agency, 1888 Century Pk. East, #1400, Los Angeles, CA 90667; (213) 277-4545

Crow, Susan & Associates, 8721 Sunset Blvd., #103, Los Angeles, CA 90669; (213) 659-1597

Cumber, L11, 6515 Sunset Blvd., #300A, Los Angeles, CA 90628; (213) 469-1919

Cunningham, Escott, Dipene & Associates, 261 South Robertson Blvd., Beverly Hills, CA 90211; (213) 855-1700

Davies Agency, Dona Lee, 3518 Cahuenga Blvd. West, #318, Los Angeles, CA 90668; (213) 850-0143

DeMille, Diana Talent Agency, 12457 Ventura Blvd., #104, Studio City, CA 91604; (818) 761-7171

Dennis, Karg, Dennis & Co., 470 San Vincente, Los Angeles, CA 90648; (213) 651-1700

Devroe Agency, Box 8629, Universal City, CA 91608; (213) 666-2666

Diamond Artists, Ltd., 9200 Sunset Blvd., #909, Los Angeles, CA 90669; (213) 278-8146

Ellas & Associates, Thomas G., 1801 Ave. of the Stars, #535, Los Angeles, CA 90667; (213) 557-1220

Elite Model Management/John Casablancas, Inc., 9255 Sunset Blvd., #1125, Los Angeles, CA 90669; (213) 274-9395

Exclusive Artists, 2501 West Burbank, #304, Burbank, CA 91505; (818) 846-0262

Farrell Talent Agency, Eileen, 10500 Magnolia Blvd., North Hollywood, CA 91601; (818) 762-6994

Felber, William, 2126 Cahuenga Blvd., Los Angeles, CA 90668; (213) 466-7629

Ferrell, Carol, 9034 Sunset Blvd., #214, Los Angeles, CA 90669; (213) 273-7511

Ferris Talent Agency, 5850 Canoga Ave., #110, Woodland Hills, CA 91367; (213) 931-8365

Fontaine Agency, Judith, 7060 Hollywood Blvd., Los Angeles, CA 90628; (213) 467-6288

Freeman-Wyckoff Agency, 6331 Hollywood Blvd., #1122, Los Angeles, CA 90628; (213) 464-4866

F.W.A.—Frances Williams, 3518 Cahuenga Blvd. West, #315, Los Angeles, CA 90668; (213) 876-2989

Garrick, Dale, 8831 Sunset Blvd., Los Angeles, CA 90669; (213) 657-2661

Gerritsen International, 8721 Sunset Blvd., #203, Los Angeles, CA 90669; (213) 659-8414

Gersh Agency, Phil, 222 North Canon Dr., Beverly Hills, CA 90210; (213) 274-6611

G.M.A., 1741 North Ivar, #119, Los Angeles, CA 90628; (213) 466-7161

Gold, Talent Agency, Harry, 8285 Sunset Blvd., #1, Los Angeles, CA 90646; (213) 654-5550

Goldin Group, 9200 Sunset Blvd., #260, Los Angeles, CA 90669; (213) 550-1001

Goldin Talent Agency, Sue, 119 North San Vicente Blvd., #104, Beverly Hills, CA 90211; (213) 659-7291

Gray, Stephan, 9025 Wilshire Blvd., #309, Beverly Hills, CA 90211; (213) 859-0344

Hecht Agency, Beverly, 8949 Sunset Blvd., Los Angeles, CA 90669; (213) 278-3544

Hunter & Assoc., Ray, 132 Lasky Dr., Beverly Hills, CA 90212; (213) 276-1137

Icon International, 207 West Alameda, #203, Burbank, CA 91502; (818) 242-2174

International Artists Agency, 6515 Sunset Blvd., #401, Los Angeles, CA 90628; (213) 463-5772

International Creative Mgmt., 8899 Beverly Blvd., Los Angeles, CA 90648; (213) 550-4000

Jard Talent, 14416 Victory Blvd., #104, Van Nuys, CA 91404; (213) 904-1304

Joseph, Held, Fond & Rix, 1717 North Highland, #414, Los Angeles, CA 90628; (213) 466-9111

Kandah Talent, 6404 Hollywood Blvd., #315, Los Angeles, CA 90628; (213) 467-7466

Kassell Agency, Carolyn, 2401 West Magnolia Blvd., Burbank, CA 91506; (818) 761-1525

Kelly-Blue, 1234 6th St., #204, Santa Monica, CA 90401; (213) 395-3548

Kjar Agency, Tyler, 8961 Sunset Blvd., #B, Los Angeles, CA 90669; (213) 278-0912

Labelle Agency, El Paso Studio 110, Santa Barbara, CA 93102; (805) 965-4575

Leonetti, Ltd., Caroline, 6526 Sunset Blvd., Los Angeles, CA 90628; (213) 463-5610

Liberty, Glennis Agency, 10845 Lindbrook Ave., #203A, Los Angeles, CA 90624; (213) 393-5078

Light Co., The, 113 North Robertson Blvd., Los Angeles, CA 90648; (213) 273-9602

Lloyd Talent Agency, Johnny, 6404 Hollywood Blvd., #219, Los Angeles, CA 90628; (213) 464-2738

Lockwood Agency, The, 470 San Vincente, #102, Los Angeles, CA 90648; (213) 655-7004

Loo Agency, Bessie, 8235 Santa Monica Blvd., #202, Los Angeles, CA 90646; (213) 650-1300

Lovell & Assoc., 1350 North Highland, Los Angeles, CA 90628; (213) 462-1672

Lund Agency, Starmakers Unlimited, 6515 Sunset Blvd., #204, Los Angeles, CA 90628; (213) 466-8280

Lynne & Reilly Artists Mgr., 6290 Sunset Blvd., Los Angeles, CA 90628; (213) 461-2828

Management One, 6464 Sunset, #590, Los Angeles, CA 90628; (213) 461-7515

Marie's Modeling & Talent Agency, Linda, 626 West Commonwealth, #H, Fullerton, CA 92632; (714) 870-7640

Marshall, Alese Model & Commercial, 24050 Vista Montana, Torrance, CA 90505; (213) 378-1223

M.A.X., 9230 Olympic Blvd., #203, Beverly Hills, CA 90212; (213) 550-8858

McMillan, Hazel, 126 North Doheny, Beverly Hills, CA 90211; (213) 276-9823

Merit Agency, The, 12926 Riverside Dr., #C, Sherman Oaks, CA 91423; (818) 986-3017

MGA/Mary Grady, 3575 Cahuenga Blvd. West, #320, Los Angeles, CA 90668; (213) 851-8872

Michaud Agency, George, 10113 Riverside Dr., Los Angeles, CA 91602; (818) 508-8314

Morris Agency, William, 151 El Camino Dr., Beverly Hills, CA 90212; (213) 274-7451

New World Artists, 8780 Sunset Blvd., Los Angeles, CA 90669; (213) 659-9737

Pacific Artists, 515 North La Cienega Blvd., Los Angeles, CA 90648; (213) 657-5990

Peterman & Assoc., 720½ Seward, Los Angeles, CA 90638; (213) 466-8664

Quo Vadis Talent, 8170 Beverly Blvd., Los Angeles, CA 90648; (213) 658-8113

Romaine Artists Mgr., Dick, 843 North Sycamore, Los Angeles, CA 90638; (213) 461-1006

Rose Agency, Jack, 6430 Sunset Blvd., Los Angeles, CA 90628; (213) 463-7300

Sanders Agency, Norah, 1100 Glendon Ave., Los Angeles, CA 90624; (213) 824-2264

Savage Agency, The, 6212 Banner Ave., Los Angeles, CA 90638 (213) 461-8316

Schaefer, Peggy, 10850 Riverside Dr., North Hollywood, CA 91602; (818) 985-5547

Schechter Co., Irv, 9300 Wilshire Blvd., #410, Beverly Hills, CA 90212; (213) 278-8070

Schoeman Talent Agency, 2600 West Victory Blvd., Burbank, CA 91505; (818) 954-0600

Schut Agency, Booh, 11350 Ventura Blvd., #206, Studio City, CA 91604; (818) 760-6669

Schwartz & Assoc., Don, 8721 Sunset Blvd., Los Angeles, CA 90669; (213) 657-8910

Screen Children's Agency, 12444 Ventura Blvd., Studio City, CA 91604; (818) 985-6131

Sherrell Agency, Ltd., Lew, 7060 Hollywood Blvd., Los Angeles, CA 90628; (213) 461-9955

Shreve Artists Manager, Dorothy, 729 West 16th, Costa Mesa, CA 92627; (714) 642-3050

Shumacker Agency, The, 10850 Riverside Dr., #410, North Hollywood, CA 91609; (818) 877-3370

Special Artists Agency, 8730 Sunset Blvd., #400, Los Angeles, CA 90669; (213) 855-1803

Sportscasting Period, 1226 Sierra Alta Way, Los Angeles, CA 90669; (213) 274-7260

Star Quality Mgmt., 885 Park Ln., Santa Barbara, CA 93108; (805) 969-9250

Star Talent, 17502 Parthenia, Northridge, CA 91320; (818) 701-7471

Stern Agency, Charles H., 9220 Sunset Blvd., Los Angeles, CA 90669; (213) 273-6890

Stevens, Steven R., 4932 Lankershim Blvd., #201, North Hollywood, CA 91601; (818) 508-6173

Stone/Masser Agency, 1052 Carol Dr., Los Angeles, CA 90669; (213) 275-9599

Strand, Winifred, 8425 West 3rd, #209, Los Angeles, CA 90648; (213) 653-8142

Studio II Artists, 12023 Ventura Blvd., Los Angeles, CA 91604; (818) 761-7855

Stunt Action, 21601 Devonshire, #208A, Chatsworth, CA 91311; (818) 709-8736

Sutton Barth & Vennari, Inc., 8322 Beverly Blvd., Los Angeles, CA 90648; (213) 653-8322

Talent Enterprises, 1607 North El Centro, #2, Los Angeles, CA 90628; (213) 462-0913

Talent Group, Inc., 8831 Sunset Blvd., Penthouse E, Suite A, Los Angeles, CA 90669; (213) 659-8072

Talent Network International, 9000 Sunset Blvd., #807, Los Angeles, CA 90669; (213) 550-0397

Tannen & Assoc., Herb, 6640 Sunset Blvd., Los Angeles, CA 90628; (213) 466-6191

Thompson, Willie, 6381 Hollywood Blvd., #450, Los Angeles, CA 90628; (213) 461-6594

Tieman, Rick, 1680 North Vine St., #700, Los Angeles, CA 90628; (213) 469-8632

Tisherman Agency, 8721 Sunset Blvd., #209, Los Angeles, CA 90669; (213) 657-1824

Top Models, 454 So. Robertson, Los Angeles, CA 90648; (213) 274-5045

Triad Artists, 10100 Santa Monica Blvd., 16th Fl., Los Angeles, CA 90667; (213) 556-2727

Universal Artists Agency, Inc., 9465 Wilshire Blvd., #616, Beverly Hills, CA 90212; (213) 278-2425

V.A.M.P., 713 East La Loma Ave., Office I, Camarillo, CA 93010; (805) 485-2001

Vannerson Ione Talent Agency, 10810 Bloomfield, North Hollywood, CA 91607; (818) 985-8725

Variety Artists Int'l. Inc., 9073 Nemo St., 3rd Fl., Los Angeles, CA 90669; (213) 858-7800

Waugh Talent Agency, Ann, 4731 Laurel Canyon Rd., #5, North Hollywood, CA 91607; (818) 980-0141

Williamson & Assoc., 932 North La Brea, Los Angeles, CA 90638; (213) 851-1881

Wood & Assoc., Billy, 5730 Lankershim Blvd., North Hollywood, CA 91601; (818) 769-1226

World Class Sports, 8530 Wilshire Blvd., #210, Beverly Hills, CA 90211; (213) 659-4603

Wright, Talent Agency, Carter, 6533 Hollywood Blvd., Los Angeles, CA 90628; (213) 469-0944

Yanez, Bob Talent Agency, 1607 North El Centro Ave., #23, Los Angeles, CA 90628; (213) 461-0298

Young Models & Talent, 9124 Sunset Blvd., Los Angeles, CA 90669; (213) 859-2491

NEW YORK

Abrams Artists & Assoc. Ltd., 420 Madison Ave., 14th Fl., New York, NY 10017; (212) 935-8980

Act 48 Management, Inc., 1501 Broadway, #1713, New York, NY 10036; (212) 354-4250

Adams, Ltd., Bret, 448 West 44 St., New York, NY 10036; (212) 765-5630

Agents For The Arts, 1650 Broadway, #306, New York, NY 10019; (212) 247-3220

Allen/Gardner Agency, 250 West 57th St., #1517–1527, New York, NY 10017; (212) 757-7475

American Talent Int., 888 7th Ave., New York, NY 10016; (212) 977-2300

Anderson Agency, Beverly, 1472 Broadway, #806, New York, NY 10036; (212) 944-7773

Andreadis Talent, 119 West 57th St., New York, NY 10019; (212) 315-0303

Baldwin-Scully Inc., 501 Fifth Ave., New York, NY 10017; (212) 922-1330 and 1697 Broadway, New York, NY 10019 (212) 581-1970

Barry Agency, 165 West 46th St., New York, NY 10036; (212) 869-9310

Beck, Bee Talent Agency Inc., 45 West 45th St., New York, NY 10036; (212) 944-5724

Beilin Agency, Peter, 230 Park Ave., New York, NY 10169; (212) 949-9119

Bloom, Ltd., J. Michael, 400 Madison Ave., New York, NY 10017; (212) 832-6900

Bonnie Kid, 25 West 36th St., New York, NY 10019; (212) 563-2141

Cunningham, Escott, Dipene, 919 3rd Ave., New York, NY 10022; (212) 832-2700

Deacy, Jane, 300 E. 75th St., 3C, New York, NY 10021; (212) 752-4865

Dilworth, Frances, 496 Kinderkamack Rd., Oradell, NJ 07649; (212) 661-0070

D.M.I. Talent Agency, Inc., 250 West 57th St., New York, NY 10019; (212) 246-4650

Foster-Fell Agency, 26 West 38th St., New York, NY 10018; (212) 944-8520

Frontier Booking Corp., 1776 Broadway, New York, NY 10019; (212) 246-1505

F.T.A. Talent Agency, 401 Park Ave. So., PH, New York, NY 10016; (212) 686-7010

Gage Group, Inc., 1650 Broadway, #406, New York, NY 10019; (212) 541-5250

Gilcrest Talent Group, 342 Madison Ave., #550, New York, NY 10173; (212) 692-9166

Grant, Peggy & Assoc., 1650 Broadway, #711, New York, NY 10019; (212) 586-1452

Henderson/Hogan Agency, Inc., 405 West 44th St., New York, NY 10036; (212) 765-5190

Henry Inc., June, 175 Fifth Ave., #801, New York, NY 10010; (212) 475-5130

Jacobson/Wilder, Inc., 419 Park Ave. So., New York, NY 10016; (212) 686-6100

Jordan Talent Agency, Inc., Joe, 200 West 57th St., #1104, New York, NY 10019; (212) 582-9003

Jovano Modeling Agency, 2320 Main St., Bridgeport, CT 06606; (203) 336-0597

Kahn Inc., Jerry, 853 Seventh Ave., New York, NY; (212) 254-7317

Kennedy Artists Rep., 881 Seventh Ave., New York, NY; (212) 675-3944

Kerin, Charles, 667 Madison Ave., New York, NY 10021; (212) 751-9191

KMA Associates, 303 West 42 St., #606, New York, NY 10036; (212) 581-4610

Kronick & Kelly Agency, Ltd., 171 Madison Ave., #1315, New York, NY 10016; (212) 684-5223

Leigh, Sanford, 527 Madison Ave., New York, NY 10022; (212) 752-4450

Lerman Talent Assocs., 37 East 28th St., #506, New York, NY 10016; (212) 889-8233

L'Etoile, 305 East 53rd St., New York, NY 10022; (212) 477-5696

L'Image Talent Group, 114 East 32nd St., #1303, New York, NY 10016; (212) 725-2424

Manning Agency, 215 Park Ave. So., #1903, New York, NY 10003; (212) 460-9800

M.E.W. Company, 370 Lexington Ave., New York, NY 10017; (212) 889-7272

MMG Enterprises Ltd., Marcia's Kids, 250 West 57th St., New York, NY 10019; (212) 246-4360

Morris Agency Wm., 1350 Ave. of Americas, New York, NY 10019; (212) 586-5100

Noble Talent, 250 West 57th St., #1501, New York, NY 10019; (212) 581-3800

Oppenheim-Christie Assoc. Ltd., 565 5th Ave., New York, NY 10017; (212) 661-4330

Perkins Talent, 1697 Broadway, New York, NY 10019; (212) 582-9511

Reich, Norman, 65 W. 55th St., #4H, New York, NY 10019; (212) 399-2881

Revelation Entertainment Co., Inc., 601 Halstead Ave., Mamaroneck, NY 10543; (212) 381-5207

Rogers, Wallace Talent, 160 East 56th St., New York, NY 10022; (212) 750-9010

Ryan, Charles Vernon, 200 West 57th St., #1405, New York, NY 10019; (212) 245-2225

Sanders Agency, Ltd., Honey, 229 West 42nd St., New York, NY 10036; (212) 947-5555

Schuller Talent, Inc., 667 Madison Ave., New York, NY 10022; (212) 758-1919

Silver, Monty, 200 W. 57th St., New York, NY 10019; (212) 765-4040

Smith Freedman & Assoc., 850 Seventh Ave., #1003, New York, NY 10019; (212) 581-4490

Thomas Agency, Inc., Michael, 305 Madison Ave., #4419, New York, NY 10165; (212) 867-0303

Tranum, Robertson & Hughes, Inc., 2 Hammarskjold Plaza, New York, NY 10017; (212) 371-7500

Van der Ver People, Inc., 225A East 59th St., New York, NY 10022; (212) 688-2880

Waters Agency, Inc., Bob, 510 Madison Ave., New York, NY 10022; (212) 593-0543

Wilhemina Artists' Representatives, Inc., 9 East 37th St., New York, NY 10016; (212) 889-9450

Zoli Mgmt., Inc., 146 East 56th St., New York, NY 10022; (212) 758-5959

ARIZONA

Ball Agency, Bobby, 808 East Osborn, Phoenix, AZ 80514; (602) 264-5007

Grissom Agency, 2909 East Grant Rd., Tucson, AZ 85716; (602) 327-5692

Netsky Talent, 4737 East Towner St., Tucson, AZ 85712 (602) 326-0118

Plaza Three Talent Agency, 1857 East Northern, Phoenix, AZ 85020; (602) 265-3000 and 5055 Broadway C-214, Tucson, AZ 85711; (602) 745-2200

Premier Talent, 4516 North 16th St., Phoenix, AZ 85016; (602) 248-8109

Sinnett & Assocs., Claire, 4425 North 24th St., Phoenix, AZ 85016; (602) 224-0822

BOSTON

Maggie, Inc., 35 Newbury Street, Boston, MA 02108; (617) 536-2639

CHICAGO

A Plus Talent Agency Corp., 666 North Lake Dr., Chicago, IL 60611; (312) 642-8151

David & Lee, 70 W. Hubbard St., #200, Chicago, IL 60610; (312) 670-4444

Johnson Talent Agency, Ltd., Susanne, 66 East Walton Pl., Chicago, IL 60611; (312) 943-8315

Marle's, Jan, Talent Agency, 100 East Ohio, #530, Chicago, IL 60611; (312) 943-0911

Medusa Talent, 132 Park Ave., Wilmette, IL 60091; (312) 251-1795

National Talent Network, Inc., 101 East Ontario St., #580, Chicago, IL 60611; (312) 280-2225

Philbin Talent Agency, 6301 North Kedvale, Chicago, IL 60646; (312) 777-5394 or 736-0711

Schucart Enterprises, Norman, 1417 Green Bay Rd., Highland Park, IL 60035; (312) 433-1113 or 433-3233

Stewart Talent Management Corp., 212 West Superior, #406, Chicago, IL 60610; (312) 661-1000

DALLAS

Blair Agency, Tanya, 3000 Carlisle, #101, Dallas, TX 75204; (214) 748-8353

Holbein & Halderman, 1350 Manufacturing, #212, Dallas, TX 75207; (214) 748-7208

Taylor Agency, Peggy, 6309 North O'Connor, #120, Dallas, TX 75039; (214) 869-1515

Townsend, J. Agency, 5925 Maple, #106, P.O. Box 36365, Dallas, TX 75235; (214) 350-4400

DENVER

Images, Inc., J.F., 3600 South Yosemite, #700, Denver, CO 80237; (303) 779-8888

Vannoy Talent, 7400 East Caley, #300, Englewood, CO 80111; (303) 771-7500

DETROIT

Advertisers Casting Service, 15326 Mack Ave., Grosse Point Park, MI 48224; (313) 881-1135
Affiliated Models, Inc., 28860 Southfield Rd., #100, Detroit, MI 48076; (313) 559-3110
Gail & Rice Productions, 11845 Mayfield, Livonia, MI 48150; (313) 427-9300
Haney, Marce Assoc., 1150 Griswold Ave., #2300, Detroit, MI 48226; (313) 961-6222
Talent Shop, 30100 Telegraph Rd., #124, Birmingham, MI 48010; (313) 644-4877

FLORIDA

Act 1 Casting Agency, 1460 Brickell Ave., #208, Miami, FL 33131; (305) 371-1371
Burns, Dott, 478 Severn, Davis Island, Tampa, FL 33606; (813) 251-5882
Cassandra Models Theatrical Agency, 635 North Hyer Ave., Orlando, FL 32803; (305) 423-7872
Coconut Grove Talent Agency, 3525 Vista Court, Miami, FL 33133; (305) 858-3002
Falcon Agency, Travis, 17070 Collins Ave., #231, Miami Beach, FL 33160; (305) 947-7957
La Mode, Inc., 11077 Biscayne, #303, Miami, FL 33161; (305) 895-4304
Marks, Herbert, 924 Lincoln Rd. Bldg., Miami Beach, FL 33140; (305) 531-8138
Marle, Irene Agency, 3212 So., Federal Hwy., Ft. Lauderdale, FL 33316; (305) 522-3262
Palm Beach/Top Models East, 155 Worth Ave., Palm Beach, FL 33480; (305) 832-7204
Polan Talent Agency, Marlan, 3798 Ravenwood Rd., Ft. Lauderdale, FL 33338; (305) 525-8351
Pommler Models, Inc., Michele, 7520 Red Road, Miami, FL 33143; (305) 763-7011
Talent Agents, The, 1528 NE 147th St., Miami, FL 33161; (305) 940-7076
Tampa Bay Talent, 3311 South Westshore Blvd., Tampa, FL 33629; (813) 831-5662

GEORGIA

Atlanta Models & Talents, Inc., 3030 Peachtree Rd., NW, #308, Atlanta, GA 30305; (404) 261-9627

Serindipity, 3130 Maple Dr., NE, #19, Atlanta, GA 30305; (404) 237-4040

HOUSTON

Agency Artists Management, 4801 Woodway, #360 West, Houston, TX 77056; (713) 623-2275

Intermedia Models & Talent, 2323 South Voss, #610, Houston, TX 77057; (713) 789-3993

Mad Hatter, Inc., Ashcroft Office Pk., 7349 Ashcroft, Bldg. B, Houston, TX 77081; (713) 995-9090

Young, Inc., Sherry, 6420 Hillcroft, #319, Houston, TX 77081; (713) 981-9236

KANSAS

Jackson Artists Corp., 7251 Lowell Dr., #200, Overland Pk., KS 66204; (913) 384-6688

NEVADA

"D" Agency, 3175 South Eastern Ave., Las Vegas, NV 89109; (702) 796-7678

Lenz Agency, 1630 Aztec, Las Vegas, NV 89109; (702) 733-6888, and 1456 East Charlston, Las Vegas, NV 89104; (702) 382-3245

Mack, Agency, Jess, 1111 Las Vegas B1, #209, South Las Vegas, NV 89104; (702) 382-2193

Morris Agency, Bobby, 1629 East Sahara Ave., Las Vegas, NV 89104; (702) 733-7575

NEW MEXICO

Mannekin Agency, 3701 San Mateo NE, Albuquerque, NM 87111; (505) 888-2935 or 888-2933

New Mexico Entertainment Agency, P.O. Box 549, Santa Fe, NM 87501; (505) 983-2330

PENNSYLVANIA

Marie McCullough Model & Talent, 8 South Hanover, Margate, NJ 08402; (215) 822-2222
Philadelphia Models, Inc., 1700 Walnut, #813, Philadelphia, PA 19103; (215) 735-9558

SAN DIEGO

Artist Management Agency, 2232 Fifth Ave., San Diego, CA 92101; (619) 233-6655
Crosby Talent Agency, Mary, 2130 Fourth Ave., San Diego, CA 92101; (619) 234-7911
Lily Talent Agency, Beatrice, 7724 Girard Ave., #201, La Jolla, CA 92037; (619) 454-3579
Patterson Agency, Janice, 3990 Old Town Ave., #103C, San Diego, CA 92110; (619) 295-9477
Real, Tina, 3108 Fifth Ave., San Diego, CA 92103; (619) 298-0544

SAN FRANCISCO

Brebner Agencies, Inc., 185 Berry St., #144, China Basin Blvd., San Francisco, CA 94107; (415) 495-6700
Demeter & Reed Ltd. Agency, 70 Zoe St., #200, San Francisco, CA 94107; (415) 777-1337
Frazer-Nicklin Agency, 4300 Stevens Creek Blvd., #140, San Jose, CA 95129; (408) 554-1055
Marechel Agency, 2421 Lombard St., San Francisco, CA 94123; (415) 563-4747
Panda Talent Agency, 3721 Heon Ave., Santa Rosa, CA 95404; (707) 576-0711
Sabina Agency, The, 278 Post St., #505, San Francisco, CA 94108; (415) 781-6424
Talents, 1400 Castro St., San Francisco, CA 94114; (415) 282-8855

TENNESSEE

Chaparral Talent Agency, P.O. Box 25, Oltewah, TN 37363; (615) 238-9790

Talent & Model Land, 1443 12th St., South, Nashville, TN 37203; (615) 385-2723

UTAH

Burton & Perkins Agency, 250 South 200 East, Salt Lake City, UT 84111; (801) 531-0090

C.T.A., 4836 South Highland, #201, Salt Lake City, UT 84109; (801) 272-9801

McCarty, 150 West 500 South, Salt Lake City, UT 84101; (801) 521-3343 or 359-9292

AFTRA OFFICES

Albany
Joe Condon, Steward
c/o Station WROW–AM
341 Northern Boulevard
Albany, NY 12204
(518) 436-4841

Doug Myers, Steward
c/o Station WTEN–TV
341 Northern Boulevard
Albany, NY 12204
(518) 436-4822

Atlanta
Kit Woods, Acting Executive
    Secretary
3110 Maple Drive, NE, Suite
    210
Atlanta, GA 30305
(404) 237-0831
(404) 237-9961

Boston
Robert Segal, Executive
    Secretary
11 Beacon Street, Suite 1000
Boston, MA 02108
(617) 742-0208
(617) 742-2688

Buffalo
John Murphy
c/o WBEN Radio
2077 Elmwood Avenue
Buffalo, NY 14207
(716) 874-4410

Chicago
Herb Neuer, Executive
    Secretary
307 North Michigan Avenue
Chicago, IL 60601
(312) 372-8081

Seymour Schriar, Esq.
29 South LaSalle Street
Chicago, IL 60603
(312) 346-0252

Cincinnati-Columbus-Dayton
John Armstrong, Executive
    Secretary
1814-16 Carew Tower
Cincinnati, OH 45202
(513) 579-8668

Cleveland
Kenneth Bichl, Executive
    Secretary
1367 East Sixth Street
The Lincoln Building, Suite
    229
Cleveland, OH 44114
(216) 781-2255

Dallas–Forth Worth
Betty Boyer, Executive
    Secretary
3220 Lemmon Avenue, Suite
    102
Dallas, TX 75204
(214) 522-2080
(214) 522-2085

Denver
Jerre Hookey, Executive
    Secretary
6825 East Tennessee, Suite
    639
Denver, CO 80224
(303) 388-4287

Detroit
Fernanda Crudo, National
    Representative
24901 North Western Highway
Heritage Plaza Office Building,
    Suite 406
Southfield, MI 48075
(313) 354-1774

Fresno
Chris Ward, President
P.O. Box 11961
Fresno, CA 93776
(209) 222-7065 (Service)
(209) 229-8918

Hawaii
Arthur L. Shotwell, President
P.O. Box 1350
745 Fort Street, #208
Honolulu, HI 96807
(808) 533-2652

Houston
Claire Gordon, Executive
    Secretary
2650 Fountainview, Suite 325
Houston, TX 77057
(713) 972-1806

Indianapolis
Irving Fink, Executive
    Secretary
Yosha & Cline
2220 North Meridian Street
Indianapolis, IN 46208
(317) 925-9200

Kansas City
Gloria Hill, Executive
    Secretary
406 West 34th Street, Suite
    206
Kansas City, MO 64111
(816) 753-4557

Los Angeles
H. Wayne Oliver, Executive
    Secretary
1717 North Highland Avenue
Hollywood, CA 90028
(213) 461-8111

Hirsch Adell, Esq.
Reich, Adell & Crost
501 Shatto Place, #100
Los Angeles, CA 90020
(213) 386-3860

Louisville
John V. Hanley, Executive
    Secretary
730 West Main Street, Suite
    470
Louisville, KY 40202
(502) 584-6594

Miami
Diane Hogan, Executive
    Secretary
1450 N.E. 123rd Street, #102
North Miami, FL 33161
(305) 891-0779

Nashville
David Maddox, Executive
    Secretary
P.O. Box 121087
1108-17th Avenue South
Nashville, TN 37212
(615) 327-2944
(615) 327-2947

New Orleans
Pauline Morgan, Executive
    Secretary
808 St. Anne
New Orleans, LA 70116
(504) 524-9903

New York
Reginald Dowell, Executive
    Secretary
1350 Avenue of the Americas
New York, NY 10019
(212) 265-7700

Mortimer Becker, Esq.
Becker & London
30 Lincoln Plaza, Mezz. Floor
New York, NY 10023
(212) 541-7070

Omaha
Mike Donovan, President
P.O. Box 31103
Omaha, NB 68131
(402) 457-6251
(402) 346-6666

Peoria
Phil Supple, President
Station WEEK
2907 Springfield Road
East Peoria, IL 61611
(309) 699-5052

Philadelphia
Glenn Goldstein, Executive
  Secretary
230 South Broad Street
10th Floor
Philadelphia, PA 19102
(215) 732-0507

Phoenix
Donald Livesay, Executive
  Secretary
5150 North 16th Street,
  #C-255
Phoenix, AZ 85016
(602) 279-9975

Pittsburgh
Dan Mallinger, Executive
  Secretary
625 Stanwix Street
The Penthouse
Pittsburgh, PA 15222
(412) 281-6767

Portland
Robert Dolton, Executive
  Secretary
915 NE Davis Street
Portland, OR 97232
(503) 238-6914

Racine-Kenosha
Ms. Irene Nelson
929-52nd Street
Kenosha, WI 53140
(414) 657-7886

Rochester
Marcia Boyd, Executive
  Secretary
One Exchange Street, Suite
  900
Rochester, NY 14614
(716) 232-5670

Sacramento-Stockton
Bob Peeler, President
8157 Canyon Oak Drive
Citrus Heights, CA 95610
(916) 722-7416

San Diego
Jacqueline Walters, Executive
  Secretary
3045 Rosecrans Street, Suite
  308
San Diego, CA 92110
(619) 222-1161

San Francisco
Donald S. Tayer, Esq.,
  Executive Secretary and
  Counsel
100 Bush Street, 15th Floor
San Francisco, CA 94104
(415) 391-7510

Schenectady
Jim Leonard, President
170 Ray Avenue
Schenectady, NY 12304
(518) 381-4836

Seattle
Carol Matt
P.O. Box 9688
158 Thomas Street
Seattle, WA 98109
(206) 728-9999

Harold Green, Esq.
MacDonald, Hoague & Bayless
Second Avenue & Cherry
  Street
Seattle, WA 98104
(206) 622-1604

St. Louis
Larry Ward, Executive
  Secretary
Paul Brown Building
818 Olive Street, Suite 1237
St. Louis, MO 63101
(314) 231-8410

Stamford
Len Gambino, Steward
c/o Station WSTC
117 Prospect Street
Stamford, CT 06901
(203) 327-1400

Twin Cities
John Kailin, Executive
　　Secretary
15 South 9th Street, Suite 485
Minneapolis, MN 55402
(612) 371-9120

Washington-Baltimore
Don Gaynor, Executive
　　Secretary
35 Wisconsin Circle, Suite 210
Chevy Chase, MD 20815
(301) 657-2560

Tom Powers, Esq.
Powers & Lewis
4201 Connecticut Avenue, NW,
　　#607
Washington, D.C. 20008
(202) 363-9740

Bernard Rubenstein, Esq.
Abato, Rubenstein & Abato
2360 Joppa Road, #308
Lutherville, MD 21093–4697
(301) 321-0990

SAG OFFICES

Arizona
3030 North Central, #301
Phoenix, AZ 85012
(602) 279-9975

Atlanta
3110 Maple Dr., NE, #210
Atlanta, GA 30305
(404) 237-9961

Boston
11 Beacon St., Rm. 1000
Boston, MA 02108
(617) 742-2688

Chicago
307 North Michigan Ave.
Chicago, IL 60601
(312) 372-8081

Cleveland*
1367 East 6th St., #229
Cleveland, OH 44114
(216) 781-2255

Dallas
3220 Lemmon Ave., #102
Dallas, TX 75204
(214) 522-2080

Denver
6825 East Tennessee Ave.,
    #639
Denver, CO 80222
(303) 388-4287

Detroit
28690 Southfield Rd.
Lathrop Village, MI 48076
(313) 559-9540

Florida
145 Madeira Ave., #317
Coral Gables, FL 33134
(305) 444-7677

Houston
2620 Fountainview, #215
Houston, TX 77057
(713) 972-1806

Kansas City
406 West 34th, #310
Kansas City, MO 64111
(816) 753-4557

Los Angeles
7750 Sunset Blvd.
Hollywood, CA 90046
(213) 876-3030

Minneapolis/*St. Paul
15 South 9th St., Suite 485
Minneapolis, MN 55402
(612) 371-9120

Nashville
1108 17th Ave. So.
Nashville, TN 37212
(615) 327-2944

Nevada
3305 West Spring Mountain
    Rd. #60
Las Vegas, NV 89102
(702) 367-8217

New Mexico
500 Indiana, SE, #C
Albuquerque, NM 87108
(505) 255-8187

New York
1700 Broadway, 18th Floor
New York, NY 10019
(212) 957-5370

Philadelphia
230 South Broad St., 10th Fl.
Philadelphia, PA 19102
(215) 545-3150

*St. Louis**
818 Olive St., #137
St. Louis, MO 63101
(314) 231-8410

San Diego
3045 Rosecrans, #308
San Diego, CA 92110
(619) 222-3996

San Francisco
100 Bush St., 26th Fl.
San Francisco, CA 94104
(415) 391-4301

*Seattle**
158 Thomas St.
Seattle, WA 98109
(206) 624-7340

Washington, D.C.
35 Wisconsin Cir., 2nd Fl.
Chevy Chase, MD 20815
(301) 657-2560

*AFTRA offices that handle SAG for their area.